LINCOLN
IN
50
BUILDINGS

DANIEL J. CODD

AMBERLEY

First published 2020

Amberley Publishing, The Hill, Stroud
Gloucestershire GL5 4EP

www.amberley-books.com

Copyright © Daniel J. Codd, 2020

British Library Cataloguing in Publication Data.
A catalogue record for this book is available from the British Library.

ISBN 978 1 4456 9163 3 (print)
ISBN 978 1 4456 9164 0 (ebook)

Typesetting by Aura Technology and Software Services, India.
Printed in Great Britain.

Contents

Key

1. Roman North Tower, Eastgate
2. Church of St Paul-in-the-Bail
3. Church of St Mary le Wigford
4. Lincoln Castle
5. Lincoln Cathedral
6. St Mary's Guildhall
7. Bishop's Palace
8. Norman House
9. Jews' Court
10. Greyfriars
11. Monks' Abbey
12. John of Gaunt's Palace
13. Exchequer Gate
14. Witch and Wardrobe
15. Whitefriars
16. The Cardinal's Hat
17. Lincoln Guildhall and Stonebow
18. High Bridge/Stokes
19. Leigh-Pemberton House
20. Lion and Snake
21. Quaker Meeting House
22. Christ's Hospital Bluecoat School
23. White Hart Hotel
24. Assembly Rooms
25. Smith, Ellison & Brown
26. Ellis' Mill
27. Theatre Royal
28. The Lawn
29. Strugglers Inn, Westgate
30. Boultham Hall, LN6 7SW
31. Sessions House
32. Lincoln Central Railway Station
33. Ruston Buildings, Waterside South
34. Le Tall's Crown Mill
35. HMP Lincoln, Greetwell Road
36. Bracebridge Hall, LN5 8QJ
37. Co-operative Building, Free School Lane
38. Lincoln County Hospital
39. Liberal Club
40. Sincil Bank Football Stadium
41. Racecourse grandstand
42. Pyewipe Junction
43. Water Tower
44. Usher Gallery
45. County Offices
46. RAF Skellingthorpe Bomb Store, LN6 0JE
47. Priory City of Lincoln Academy, LN6 0EP
48. Lincoln Drill Hall
49. The Engine Shed
50. Waterside Shopping Centre

Introduction

One way to appreciate the development of Lincoln is to consider it as a sequence of eras, each characterised by either economic decline or prosperity.

Lincoln's earliest permanent settlers were Iron Age *Corieltauvi* tribespeople. Then, in the first century AD, came the Romans, who established Lincoln as one of the finest cities in their conquered nation. Lincoln deteriorated sharply during the Anglo-Saxon period following the Roman departure, but then improved greatly after colonisation by the mercantile Danes. In the eleventh century Norman invaders gave us the castle and the cathedral, and in medieval times Lincoln prospered immensely thanks in part to the cloth industry, becoming a place of merchants, waterborne trade and royal parliaments. The city declined

Brayford Pool c. 1900.

again from the late fourteenth century: initially aggravated by extensive flooding in the lower town and a devastating plague throughout 1348–9, it was gradually eclipsed by other places as it lost its royal privileges. Local trade was further impacted by a violent private feud, precipitated by Sir Walter Tailboys assaulting Lincoln with 160 armed men in 1411, and by 1447 the city was described as impoverished, with many merchants and craftsmen having withdrawn. Over generations Lincoln dwindled to the rank of an agricultural market town. It suffered a prolonged outbreak of plague from 1630 and a pummelling during the civil wars of the 1640s; Daniel Defoe described it in the early eighteenth century as 'an *antient*, ragged, decay'd, and still decaying City; it is so full of the ruins of monasteries and religious houses.' From the 1740s onwards, however, Lincoln's fortunes revitalised, with the reopening of the Fossdyke Canal and the gradual development of the Brayford Pool into an inland port. By the early 1800s the Brayford's banks were lined with wharves, mills, breweries and warehouses. Next, helped by the introduction of the railway, the city burgeoned into a showpiece of Victorian industrialisation. Iron-founding, the production of agricultural machinery, engineering and (during the First World War) aircraft and munitions manufacture were among Lincoln's most important trades for generations of apprentices. Today, this has declined, but has been balanced by retail, tourism and higher education opportunities.

Virtually every stage of this development can be observed in Lincoln's buildings.

Lincoln originated as an Iron Age settlement on the margin of the Brayford Pool, then vastly bigger than it is today. Lincoln's original name has been reconstructed as *Lindon*, derived from the Welsh '*llyn*' meaning pool or lake. The settlement's extent is unknown, although traces of rude timber dwellings and pottery dating to *c*. 100 BC have been unearthed east of today's Brayford Pool, on what was then probably a small defendable island. The *Corieltauvi* tribespeople inhabiting

2,500-year-old boat found in the River Witham. (Photo courtesy of The Collection)

Lindon lived by farming, hunting, fishing and trading. They were active in the vicinity centuries before 100 BC, however – as evidenced by the hollowed-out tree trunks used as boats that have been discovered in the Witham Valley in their hundreds. The famous Witham Shield, a masterpiece of prehistoric British art, was also found in the River Witham, just east of Lincoln. Dated to *c*. 300 BC, it was possibly cast in as a votive offering by a wealthy local chieftain.

Within around four years of the Roman invasion of Britain in AD 43, Lincolnshire was conquered. Troops of the 9th Legion easily displaced Lindon's inhabitants and an early Roman fort was probably set up on the slopes near the Brayford. However, the strategically minded legionnaires announced their intention of staying for good with the erection of a timber fortress on the commanding summit of the overlooking ridge. There is as yet no evidence the *Corieltauvi* tribespeople resisted, and they may have simply become absorbed into Roman society.

The Roman's military fortress on the hilltop was completed *c*. AD 60. In the Bail, in what was once a courtyard belonging to the legionary headquarters, there can today be found a 45-foot-deep well that served the complex. The well's shaft may have been dug by the 9th Roman Legion. (This well continued in use until *c*. 1644, when it was possibly deliberately polluted by Parliamentary troops during the civil wars.)

The 9th Legion was replaced by the 2nd Legion around AD 71, who occupied the fortress for around eight years. However, between AD 80–90 the garrison became a civilian settlement of high status for retired Roman soldiers. They called it *Lindum Colonia* (*Lindum* Latinized from the native 'Lindon') – or, as we know it today, *Lin-coln*.

In a single bound Lincoln had come into recorded history, and here we begin our look at the city's fifty buildings.

This well may have been constructed by the 9th Legion.

The 50 Buildings

1. Roman North Tower, Eastgate

Perhaps the nearest thing left resembling a Roman *building* is the ruin of the North Tower on Eastgate. This ancient stone structure formed part of the eastern gateway into Roman Lincoln. It replaced an original wooden gateway established *c.* AD 60 by the 9th Legion, which was itself strengthened *c.* 71 by the 2nd Legion. What we see today is the base of a semicircular tower dating to the early 200s, when it was rebuilt in monumental style. A doorway into the tower and the start of a flight of steps leading to the upper stories can be seen. The North Tower was one of a pair, which flanked two arched gateways: the remains of the South Tower are under the ground, across the road.

The gateway remained in use long after the Romans left; it was still standing *c.* 1130 when Bishop Alexander of Lincoln was granted royal permission to convert it into lodgings. Over time it became mostly lost, and the North Tower wasn't properly excavated until 1963–66.

Lincoln's most conspicuous Roman ruin, however, is Newport Arch, which was begun in the early third century and originally formed *Lindum's* Northern Gate. At its grandest the arch consisted of a central carriageway entrance for horse-drawn traffic, with pedestrian arches either side. Its scale can be appreciated when it is learned that what remains is merely part of the gateway's inner wall; there was

North Tower, Eastgate.

Above: Newport Arch.

Right: Remnant of one of Newport Arch's towers.

also formerly an outer wall, pulled down in the late 1700s. The structure also had a substantial upper storey and was flanked by semicircular towers. On the western side, easily overlooked, is the subterranean base of one such tower, evidencing that the Roman street level was significantly lower. Newport Arch is more famous than Eastgate's remains because to this day traffic continues to pass beneath it.

From its original plateau, *Lindum* began to spread downhill, beyond its south gate (between 25 and 44 Steep Hill), to utilize the river for commercial purposes. The Romans also brought technology, constructing a sophisticated aqueduct, or earthenware pipe, for channelling water into upper Lincoln from a spring called Roaring Meg, 1.7 miles to the north. How, or even whether, the aqueduct worked is a mystery, but *Lindum* must have got its water from somewhere other than wells and rainwater, for its public baths to have functioned. Along East Bight there can be seen the site of a Roman reservoir, enclosed behind a remaining portion of the northern defensive wall, which would have connected with Newport Arch.

In the late 1800s excavations discovered the shafts of Doric columns running in a straight line for 275 feet along the street called Bailgate. The columns would have formed the eastern colonnade of the Forum (or administrative, religious and commercial hub) of *Lindum*. These remains can no longer be seen, but circular setts in the road mark their position. Amazingly, the massive Mint Wall, West Bight, is a remnant portion of this complex's north wall, forming part of the *basilica*, or town-hall equivalent. By the late fourth century timber churches may have existed in the Roman Forum, with the aforementioned well being used for the first Christian baptisms.

The Collection Museum today displays numerous tombstones of those who lived in *Lindum*. These include Gaius Valerius of the 9th Legion; Flavius the Greek (who may have been a doctor); and Claudia Crysis, a wealthy member of the city's Roman elite who died aged ninety.

Exactly when the Romans abandoned *Lindum* as part of their withdrawal from Britain is unclear, although during the reign of Emperor Honorius (393–423) is probable.

2. Church of St Paul-in-the-Bail

The Dark Ages followed Rome's withdrawal, a violent time of historical obscurity that bred legends. Around 475 Lincoln may have been captured by the Saxon warlord Hengist, and then reconquered by Ambrosius Aurelianus, a Romano-British leader, in 487. According to the imaginative Geoffrey of Monmouth, 'Lindocolinum' was besieged by the Saxons under Cerdic, but relieved by King Arthur around 501, who slaughtered them in battle. Geoffrey tells us thousands of Saxons died, suggesting many drowned in the Witham while fleeing.

By the sixth century, parts of the town had become largely deserted, with trade on the river falling silent. However, when Lincoln (and the surrounding Anglo-Saxon kingdom of Lindsey) began to fall under the alternating control of Northumbria and Mercia's royal houses, it slowly came to life again.

Around 627 Lincoln was visited by Bishop Paulinus, the legendary missionary who had converted King Edwin of Northumbria to Christianity. Paganism having taken hold in Britain, Paulinus converted Lincoln's *Praefectus* (official) Blecca and his household in a ceremony near the River Trent. A beautiful stone church was established following his visit, which very likely sat in the Roman Forum.

The Venerable Bede (d. 735) recorded that by his time this church was in ruins, probably 'thrown down by enemies', although every year miraculous cures were reported at the site. But incredibly this primitive structure appears to have been the

Above: Footprint of
St Paul-in-the-Bail's
church.

Right: Grave markers
preserved at the site.

first in a sequence of churches dedicated to Paulinus (St Paul) that sat in the Bail –
including one that collapsed in 1301, a small Georgian version and a much larger
Victorian model built to cater for Lincoln's by then rapidly growing population.

In 1971 this most recent Church of St Paul-in-the-Bail was pulled down – and
nothing remains of it now. Certain inscribed gravestones have been retained as
features at the site.

The parish of St-Paul-in-the-Bail became amalgamated with the neighbouring
parish of St Mary Magdalene, whose church still looks over Bailgate and Castle
Square. Although of Saxon origins, the present Church of St Mary Magdalene
'only' dates to 1317, and was restored in 1695 following its partial destruction in
the civil wars fifty years earlier. The church is affectionately called 'Bodley's Little
Gem' following its further restoration by G. F. Bodley in 1882.

St Paul's survival is therefore reflected in this 'adopted' church.

3. Church of St Mary le Wigford

In 754 Lincoln – then governed by an Anglo-Saxon ealdorman – is said to have
been ravaged by the army of one Bernwulf. In 869 the town and surrounding area
was assaulted and plundered again with great carnage by organised marauders
under Ivar and Hubba. This reflected a new threat, that of the Danes, or Vikings,
who since the end of the eighth century had begun constantly landing, attacking
and settling in different parts of the country, including Lindsey. Possession of
England switched between Anglo-Saxon kings and Viking invaders, and periods
of relative stability became replaced by violent upheaval.

Danish invaders established themselves in Lincoln around 876. However,
Lincoln – having become a Scandinavian colony with a dual population – actually
prospered during this uncertain period, thanks to the Danes' mercantile expertise.
Viking longboats plying the waterways would have been a common sight.

During their occupation the suburb of Wigford developed along modern
High Street, outside the existing city limits, in what became virtually a separate
community, with its own common (the South Common). The Moot Stone –
meeting place of Lincoln's court of burgesses in the time of Danish rule – was on
High Street, between Corporation Street and Silver Street.

Danesgate is a telling road name, '*gata*' being Danish for 'street', implying that
when the Danes were masters of Lincoln they resided chiefly in that quarter;
although it should not be assumed all Lincoln's old streets ending in 'gate' have
Danish origins. For instance, Bargate and Little Bargate Street are so named after
defensive gatehouses that once guarded High Street at the Sincil Dike. Nothing
remains of the gatehouses now but old sketches suggest them to have been later
Norman-era.

Viking rule in Lincoln ended in 918, although many Danish families settled in
to become good Lincolnshire freeholders and traders.

The Church of St Mary le Wigford on High Street has existed since this era. Dated to *c.* 980, the original church consisted of a timber nave and chancel, which became strengthened in stone and redeveloped over the centuries. The church's tower possibly dates to the early eleventh century, and inserted in its western exterior is a reused Roman tombstone, dedicated by one Eirtig, who may have been a merchant at the time the tower was constructed.

St Mary le Wigford's Church holds the record for the longest period of unbroken Christian service in Lincoln, being one of only two still-standing churches fit for public worship after the civil wars of the 1640s. (The other was eleventh-century St Peter-at-Gowts Church further along High Street.)

The church boasts many historical artefacts, including 'Old Kate', the Tudor Lincoln Curfew Bell; a memorial stone to a Tudor sheriff of Lincoln; and the Grantham Tomb (see elsewhere). On its western edge is the Conduit head, which from the time of King Henry VIII was fed by a pipeline from a local water source and served as a water tank. It was built around 1540 from fragments of the de Kyme Chantry at the White Friary (which stood a little to the south-west at St Marks). The Tudor antiquarian Leland recorded that the Conduit's boundary wall was decorated by the tomb covers of a merchant, Ranulphus de Kyme, and his wife, who were benefactors of both the church and the friary. These tomb covers are now inside the church; the Conduit itself ceased functioning in the early twentieth century.

St Mary le Wigford and the Conduit.

An inscribed Roman stone was incorporated in the tower.

4. Lincoln Castle

With the exception of the sacking of Lincoln by new Danish plunderers in 1016 (who were driven off), the years immediately before the Norman invasion were mostly peaceful for the town. But the advancement of William the Conqueror into northern England saw him establish a strategic fortification here in 1068, situated uphill where there was a strong defensive position. One hundred and sixty-six dwellings were pulled down to make way for this castle. In 2013 the remains of a small pre-Norman stone chapel, possibly pulled down during William's ruthless land clearance, were discovered at the site. The excavations also revealed the skeleton of someone of immense importance who had died between 1035 and 1070. Whoever he was, he was buried in a special limestone sarcophagus alongside others – including a youth who appeared to have suffered a stab wound.

The original fortification utilized the former Roman defences. It probably consisted of a conical motte, or mound, at the south-west (where the Lucy Tower is), supporting a wooden tower. This formed part of a wider enclosure consisting of ditch and ramparts, otherwise the bailey. Since that time the immediate area has been called the Bail. The castle as seen today probably made the transition to stone in the late eleventh century, quickly developing into a formidable military and administrative stronghold.

It also functioned as a gaol. An early prisoner was a young Saxon priest, Turgot, held by William the Conqueror as a hostage in 1069 until he managed to bribe his gaolers and escape to Norway. Moreover, the castle saw actual warfare. In the mid-twelfth century England was torn by a civil war so destructive it became called 'The Anarchy', between King Henry I's daughter, Empress Matilda, and his nephew, Stephen of Blois. Lincoln – still utilizing Roman defensive walls at this point – was held by Empress Matilda in 1140 until Stephen besieged the city and she was forced to escape. Although Stephen left a small garrison at the castle, it was next seized using a clever ruse by Earl Ranulf of Chester, Stephen's most determined opponent and a supporter of Matilda. Over Christmas Stephen re-entered the city, and again besieged the castle. He was in turn attacked by a pro-Matilda relief army led by the Earl of Gloucester, leading to a battle just west of the castle on 2 February 1141. In the end Stephen's support deserted him, and he – 'foaming like a mad boar' and striking anyone who came near him with a battle-axe – was knocked down with a stone and taken prisoner. Lincoln's citizens were slaughtered for supporting Stephen: many ran to the Brayford to flee by flimsy boats, which in turn tipped over, drowning huge numbers of people.

Stephen was released in a prisoner swap, and by Christmas 1143 he was back in Lincoln, again besieging Lincoln Castle. This he broke off, however, after eighty of his workmen suffocated in a catastrophic trench accident on its western side. Eventually recovering the castle by political stratagem, rather than war, Stephen spent Christmas 1147 here; but after his departure Ranulf of Chester attempted to regain the city. However, Ranulf was decisively defeated in another battle outside Newport Arch during which his chief commander was slain. The civil war ended in 1153.

Conflict visited Lincoln again the following century. In 1216, as part of the First Barons' War, Lincoln was taken by disloyal barons and the French. By May 1217 Lincoln Castle was still being besieged by 'Capetians' – forces backing Louis Capet of France's claim to the English throne. Throughout, however, the castle remained unconquered thanks to its legendary armed defence in the name of King

Castle East Gate.

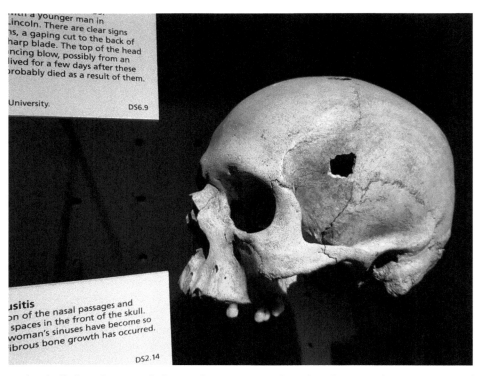

...th a younger man in Lincoln. There are clear signs ...s, a gaping cut to the back of ...harp blade. The top of the head ...ncing blow, possibly from an lived for a few days after these ...robably died as a result of them.

University.   DS6.9

...usitis ...on of the nasal passages and spaces in the front of the skull. woman's sinuses have become so fibrous bone growth has occurred.

DS2.14

Male skull found west of the castle, a victim of medieval war. (Photo courtesy of The Collection)

Henry III by the Royalist Nicola de la Haie, Constable of Lincoln Castle since her husband's death. (Nicola had, in fact, defended the castle successfully already, in 1191 against the army of William de Longchamp.)

On 19 May deliverance arrived in the shape of the forces of the Earl of Pembroke, the regent during Henry III's minority, who breached the city's defensive walls through Newport Arch and wrought carnage among the 'Capetians'. Pembroke's victory was aided by an elite detachment of crossbowmen, smuggled into the castle through a postern on its western side, who slaughtered the enemy and their horses indiscriminately from the battlements. Eventually, the rebel leader, the Count of Perche, was killed by a knight who stabbed him in the eye after he was surrounded near the cathedral. Upon this, the rebel battalions took flight, sustaining great losses, and (the citizens having supported the wrong side) the king's soldiers plundered Lincoln, including its churches and cathedral, without mercy.

In February 1643 a Royalist squire, William Chaldwell of Thorganby, was thrown into a 'nasty stinking place called the Witch Hole' at the castle by Lincoln's Parliamentary administrators. Chaldwell's wife Anne voluntarily submitted to imprisonment, to tend to her husband, but Welden – the castle's tyrannical governor – later had her thrown out of the castle and into the cold. Dressed only in her nightclothes, Anne Chaldwell's treatment was so brutal that she died that July.

Tomb of Nicola de la Haie, Lincoln's legendary defender, at Swayton.

The 'Witch Hole' is likely a reference to the earlier incarceration at the castle of the infamous Belvoir Witches before their execution at Lincoln on 11 March 1619.

These civil wars were also the last time Lincoln Castle saw battle. By spring 1644 it was controlled by Royalists, but on 3 May the Earl of Manchester's 'roundhead' Parliamentary army entered via Canwick and seized the lower town. The Royalists fled uphill, but three days later (after having to wait for heavy rain to pass) the earl's forces stormed the castle in a ferocious assault that threw its defenders into panic. Twelve of the earl's troops were killed, some by rocks thrown down upon them from the castle walls, but ultimately the Parliamentarians killed or captured around 1,000 opponents. On 7 March, the victorious roundheads ransacked upper Lincoln, vandalizing the cathedral and murdering in the process a man called Price, who had defended the castle.

The castle was rendered indefensible, meaning that when the Royalists came to retake the city in 1648 the Bishop's Palace was where the 100 remaining Parliamentarians made their last stand (see elsewhere). During their short-lived reoccupation of Lincoln, the Royalists freed all prisoners, political or otherwise, from the castle – including various women charged with child murder. A few days later, having been plundered and left to its fate, Lincoln was reconquered

Buck's 1727 detail of Lucy Tower from (where is now) Drury Lane.

conclusively by Parliamentary forces. It remained under something approaching a dictatorship until the monarchy was restored.

The castle's early gaol buildings have come and gone, leaving no traces. But we know in the eighteenth century it incarcerated debtors, Jacobite rebels, and the very worst of criminals. For example, in 1769 two prisoners – one awaiting trial for a mass murder at Normanby – kicked to death a sheep stealer 'in the pit' for being an informer. Two attempted mass breakouts in 1785 led to some felons being chained by their *necks* to the wall. Prison reform saw the completion of a new Georgian Gaol and Governor's House in 1788.

In the 1820s the south-east tower (dating from the time of King Stephen) was modified by John Merryweather, the prison's governor from 1799. This was as much for stargazing as spotting escaping inmates, and earned it the name 'the Observatory Tower'. During the Second World War, tin-hatted civil defence volunteers scanned the skies with binoculars from this tower, looking for enemy aircraft.

The Georgian Gaol was significantly redeveloped and extended in the 1840s for the 'Separate System' regime. Its unique chapel reflects the harsh reality of this, with each uncomfortable pew enclosed in a coffin-shaped booth so that the criminal within could only focus on the preacher at the pulpit, and not corrupt their neighbour. Today, only the front section of the Georgian Gaol remains, the rest being demolished to make way for the Victorian Prison.

On the north-east corner, Cobb's Hall was fitted up as Lincoln's place of execution in 1815. Among the casualties, four died 'on the new drop' in full view of the people below in 1818, while in 1823 three men were hanged there

Above: Left to right: Victorian Prison, Observatory Tower and Lucy Tower.

Below: 'Separate system' chapel interior.

for sodomy – one of the last times this punishment happened in England. The ironwork that fastened the gallows structure on top of Cobb's Hall can still be seen. From 1829 the early twelfth-century polygonal Lucy Tower – named after a formidable medieval sheriff and landowner, Lucy de Taillebois – became the graveyard of prisoners who died within the castle, by execution or natural causes. Pitifully basic tombstones can still be seen within. The last public execution occurred at Cobb's Hall in 1859, but afterwards hangings continued within the castle grounds near the steps to Lucy Tower.

Yellow-bricked lodgings, built in 1810 for visiting judges, are immediately by the castle's East Gate. Since 1878 the castle has ceased to be used as a prison, however; although the Crown Court – built in the 1820s in the Gothic Revival style for the twice-yearly Lincolnshire Assizes – is still a working court in the grounds.

Among the antiquities at the castle is Lincoln's Eleanor cross. This was erected by King Edward I in the thirteenth century at the foot of Cross O'Cliff Hill, close to the Gilbertine priory of St Catherine, in memory of his wife's body being embalmed there by the nuns during its journey home to London. The priory was pulled down in the 1700s. The castle also holds a priceless copy of the Magna Carta presented to the Bishop of Lincoln in 1215. This historic English charter, forced upon King John by the barons, is one of only four copies taken contemporarily that survive. It was rediscovered in 1810 after being forgotten for centuries.

Above: Grave in Lucy Tower of Priscilla Biggadyke, the first female hanged under the Private Executions Act.

Left: Remains of Lincoln's Eleanor cross.

5. Lincoln Cathedral

Around 1072 William the Conqueror granted permission for Bishop Remigius de Fécamp, who held the vast bishopric of Dorchester-on-Thames, to move the episcopal seat to Lincoln, and build a magnificent new cathedral. Romanesque in style, with rounded arches, the building's dominating location was befitting of such a worthy project. What is more, it seems clear that Lincoln Cathedral was built on the site of an earlier Saxon church, St Mary Magdalene's, which sat somewhere near the present Nave and had its burial ground in (what is now) the Morning Chapel.

Remigius' cathedral was smaller than the one we see today. It was completed in 1092, but Remigius – having become the first Bishop of Lincoln – died days before its consecration. His successor as bishop, Robert Bloet, dedicated the church to the Blessed Virgin Mary.

Lincoln, with its wooden houses, was prey to fire in these times. One, around 1110, nearly consumed the town, while another in 1123 killed a great many people. It may have been this second event which, according to Geraldus, caused a mass of material to fall on Remigius' tomb in the cathedral and break it in two.

Lincoln Cathedral West Front.

Then again, it might have been an earthquake said to have occurred *c.* 1142. Either way, the broken tombstone in the Nave was long argued, questionably, to be evidence of this. Remigius' remains were transferred in the late thirteenth century to a tomb beside the High Altar.

Another earthquake, on 15 April 1185, split the cathedral from top to bottom. Hugh of Avalon, who was enthroned as bishop the following year, set about reconstructing and greatly enlarging the battered building in the new Gothic style.

Hugh is arguably Lincoln's most famous bishop, a powerful and respected figure who was unafraid of the tempestuous monarchs of the day. Stories about him are legion, not least that of the famous swan of Stow, a huge bird which protected him like a guard dog and evidenced an almost supernatural devotion to him. After his death in 1200 in London, Hugh's coffin was borne into Lincoln by royalty to its place of interment inside the cathedral.

In 1205 murder desecrated Lincoln Cathedral when a sub-dean was assassinated before St Peter's altar (in the South East Transept). William de Bramford was killed by a dismissed vicar, who was himself immediately killed by cathedral servants before his remains were unceremoniously thrown out of the holy building.

Much of Lincoln Cathedral as we see it today was begun by Hugh of Avalon, and carried on by his successors and devotees, William de Blois, Hugh de Wells, and Bishop Grosseteste. During this redevelopment, three workmen were killed and the cathedral much damaged when the Central Tower collapsed in 1237.

Interestingly, Grosseteste did not pull the remnant Norman-era work down, leaving the West Front with Remigius' five original deep recesses. The way the West Front developed allows us to compare two architectural styles – Norman and Early English – side by side. Further expansion followed immediately after Grosseteste's death, with the development *c.* 1280 of the Angel Choir and St Hugh's Shrine to the east. (This is an example of architecture from the Early Decorated period.) This became necessary on account of the number of pilgrims who visited the cathedral after Hugh's canonization in 1220. Around 1363, thieves stole his skull from a head shrine, stripping it of the gold, silver and gems which decorated it, before throwing it in a field – where, according to Henry Knighton, a crow watched over it until it was recovered and returned to the cathedral. The thieves were hanged. A statue on the southernmost pinnacle of the West Front represents Hugh blessing Lincolnshire.

Lincoln Cathedral is more formally the Cathedral Church of the Blessed Virgin Mary. In this building, Lincoln has inherited a world-renowned architectural treasure that possesses many features and qualities. Built of honey-coloured Lincolnshire oolite limestone, the cathedral seems to change tone as the light varies, while its three soaring towers – so often slightly veiled in mist – dominate every vista, near and far. Inside, the aisled Nave is a breathtaking example of Early English Gothic architecture, 80 feet from stone floor to vaulting. In fact, each area of the cathedral can be identified by its spectacular overhead vaults:

West Front from street level.

over St Hugh's Choir, for example, is a complicated system of rib-like arches, nicknamed 'the Crazy Vaults of Lincoln'. Further east, the Angel Choir is so named because of the thirty carved angels enriching the spandrels. Here, the Great East Window's eight lights bathe St Hugh's Shrine, and much of the rest of this part, in a colourful light. Other huge windows, circular and intricate, illuminate the North and South Transepts, and are called the Dean's Eye and Bishop's Eye, respectively. On the south exterior, the rare Galilee Porch (c. 1250) projects from the South Transept, while further east on this side the Judgement Porch was the original pilgrim's entrance into the Angel Choir. It is now protected by beautiful statues of the Virgin and Child, and Our Lord in Glory.

After its main period of development, the cathedral still faced threats. In 1540 St Hugh's Shrine was despoiled by Henry VIII's commissioners, and the saint's remains seem to have been spirited away to an unknown location. In 1609 the building was damaged by fire, and in 1644 a Royalist pamphlet reported 'Cromwell's barbarous crew' had stabled their horses inside and committed extensive vandalism. Oliver Cromwell himself apparently considered

Above left: Great East Window. In the foreground, a table-tomb marks where Hugh of Avalon was initially buried.

Above right: 'Crazy Vaults' of St Hugh's Choir.

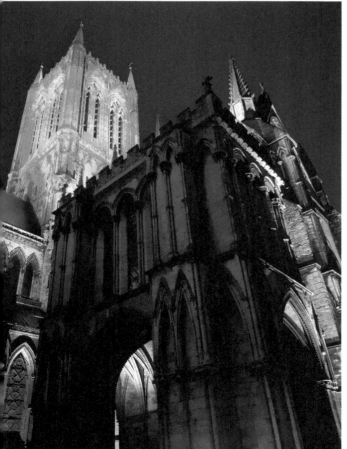

Left: Galilee Porch, stately entrance for bishops from the palace. The Central Tower is behind.

(then rejected) a proposal to demolish the entire building and use the materials to build several smaller churches. The damage continued under Cromwell's 'Protectorate': the diarist John Evelyn visited Lincoln in 1654 and observed how men with axes and hammers had lately plundered the building of brass and metal, 'not sparing even the monuments of the dead'. Twenty years later the prominent architect Wren was instrumental in redesigning the cathedral's Library.

From around 1311, Lincoln Cathedral was the world's tallest building until the Central Tower's spire came crashing down during a storm in 1548; spires on the two western towers were taken down in 1807. The Central Tower – the tallest of the three at 271 feet – today houses a bell called 'Great Tom'. It is not the original. The present Great Tom 'only' dates to 1835, its predecessor (then housed in one of the smaller towers) having been discovered to be cracked on Christmas Day 1828 following a worrying change in its tone.

Both the interior and exterior are decorated with a multitude of beautiful statues, sculptured friezes and grotesques, but one outdoes them all. In 1898 the writer Arnold Frost recorded for posterity an odd piece of folklore concerning two imps taken by their elemental friend the wind to the cathedral, one of which became turned to stone by the holy magnificence of the interior. Since then, this imp has occupied a pillar in the Angel Choir, sitting cross-legged and grinning wickedly, just as he was when petrified all those centuries ago. The story is one of the most famous legends in Britain, and the imp has become emblematic of Lincoln generally.

Finally, in the cathedral's grounds can be found a magnificent statue of the Lincolnshire poet Alfred, Lord Tennyson (d. 1892), and his wolfhound Karenina. Unveiled in 1905, following the removal of several houses on the spot, it was sculpted by Tennyson's old friend George Watts, who did not live to see it erected, having died the year before.

View from the Central Tower, looking towards the castle.

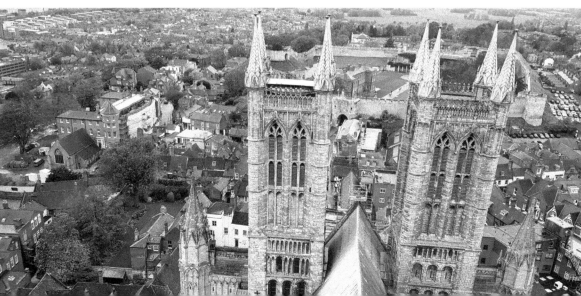

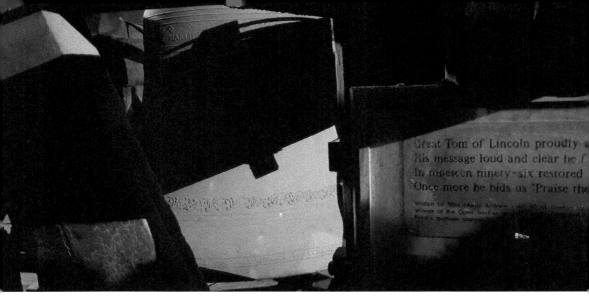

Great Tom of Lincoln proudly
His message loud and clear he f
In nineteen ninety-six restored
Once more he bids us "Praise the

Written by Mrs Marie Andrews
Winner of the Open Section
had a quatrain compos

Above: Great Tom.

Left: Lincoln Imp.

Below: Lincoln Cathedral dominates the town's skyline for miles.

6. St Mary's Guildhall

This building is readily recognized on modern High Street from its Norman architecture. It was built in the mid-twelfth century, as Lincoln developed into a flourishing, wealthy place of cloth manufacture, trade and royal esteem. Possibly it originated as a provincial palace for Henry II, who had himself crowned a second time over Christmas 1157 at Wigford. Later, it was used for royal wine storage.

In July 1537 Baron Hussey of Sleaford was beheaded in Lincoln's castle yard, amid great public disorder. He had been implicated in an uprising against Henry VIII called the Pilgrimage of Grace. An oft-repeated tradition alleges he was dragged violently out a bow window at St Mary's Guildhall to his death, although the Tudor traveler Leland suggests a house on the *west* side of High Street was the place. Banks' *Baronage* (1808) states that Hussey's stone coffin was discovered 'some few years since' in a renovated Lincoln garden, but workmen demolished it to fill up a disused well.

Leland recorded the building as 'a fair Guild *Haul*', and today it is most famous as the former hall of the Great Gild of St Mary, the city's leading socio-religious guild, or association of power-brokers, prominent citizens and merchants. The Gild of St Mary was one of the oldest and richest of numerous city guilds. The Guildhall was their meeting place from 1252 until 1545. In the early 1600s it became a Bluecoat school, before this relocated uphill. Over time the Guildhall became known as John of Gaunt's Stables, from that influential prince, soldier and statesman supposedly having in the fourteenth century a palace opposite, where a street bears his name.

The richly moulded arched stone entrance still looks out onto busy High Street, but the Guildhall lost both an upper storey and its high estate long ago. Preserved and visible beneath its floor is a cartwheel-rutted section of the Roman Fosse Way that linked Exeter to Lincoln.

St Mary's Guildhall.

7. Bishop's Palace

Approached from the thirteenth century Vicars' Court off Minster Yard via two stone gateways, there lie the ruins of the Bishop's Palace. The inner gateway has been rebuilt, but the outer still bears the arms of its builder, Bishop Smyth, who died in office in 1514.

The foundation of the palace itself is commonly ascribed to Lincoln's 4th bishop, Robert de Chesney, on account of a charter given to him by King Henry II *c.* 1155, although it is possible a bishop's residence existed in some form on the site earlier that century. Development of the palace continued under subsequent medieval bishops, who in the late twelfth century introduced the Lower East Hall (now subterranean, its stone bays resembling a cellar) and the dominating West Hall. In the 1430s Bishop Alnwick built the three-storey inner gate tower with its square-headed doorway and embattled oriel window. Within, there is a remarkable carving of a ship etched on the wall – ancient graffiti preserved to this day.

In 1536 rebels supporting the Pilgrimage of Grace entered the palace and vandalized it, while in 1541 King Henry VIII and his bride Catherine Howard were entertained there by Bishop Longland. Catherine would later be executed in London for treason and adultery, one of her alleged indiscretions traditionally said to have been committed in a cellar at the Bishop's Palace.

After Henry VIII suppressed the monasteries, going so far as to initiate the looting of the adjacent cathedral in 1540 and 1548, the palace's splendor fell steadily into decline. It was abandoned as a residence in the early seventeenth century, and the end came on 30 June 1648 during the civil wars. Royalists under Sir Philip Monkton set the palace on fire during their short-lived occupation of Lincoln, flushing out an enclave of Parliamentarians holed up there and killing one of them in the process. Afterwards, it was plundered, burnt and left in ruins.

Ruins of the Bishop's Palace, including the Alnwick Tower.

Today, the Alnwick Tower's interior walls bear a reddish hue – scorched evidence of the wartime blaze.

The palace's old stone was used to repair the cathedral in 1726. The following year one Dr Nelthorpe obtained a twenty-one-year-lease of the site, and began rebuilding or enlarging a dwelling house on the western side of the grounds. In the mid-1880s this was remodelled and enlarged to make a new palace for Bishop King, complete with a bishop's chapel that emerged from the West Hall's remains. This Victorian palace is known as Edward King House. The diocese is still administered from here, although it only served as the bishops' residence until 1945.

The original Bishop's Palace remains a picturesque ruin.

8. Norman House

Jews had begun to settle in Lincoln during the reign of King Stephen, encouraged by the town's extensive trade and the royal castle to which they might look for protection. England's most powerful Jewish inhabitant was Aaron of Lincoln (1130–86), an immensely wealthy moneylender richer even than Stephen's successor, King Henry II. The king and Bishop of Lincoln were among those who borrowed extensively from Aaron to build castles, cathedrals and monasteries.

The stone house on the corner of Christ's Hospital Terrace, Steep Hill, is associated with him and called Aaron's House, or alternatively (the) Norman House, although Aaron did business in nine shires and the connection is today believed incorrect. The house's first known inhabitant was Joceus of York, while Aaron possibly lived in the Bail when in Lincoln.

Below left: Norman House.

Below right: Eighteenth-century boundary stone at Norman House: the point where the town council's authority ended and the castle constable's began.

The Norman House dates to *c.* 1170 and its early exterior features are preserved, including the re-set first-floor window, while inside there is an extensive barrel-vaulted cellar reached by a narrow, winding stone staircase. It was built with walls of enormous thickness, and is proudly spoken of in Lincoln as one of Europe's oldest inhabited houses. Today, it is home to the Bookstop Café and Imperial Tea & Coffee.

9. Jews' Court

According to a questionable account by Matthew of Paris (d. 1259), around August 1255 Lincoln's Jewish community stole away an eight-year-old boy, Hugh, who lived at the bottom of Steep Hill, ritually killing him and hiding his corpse down a well.

However the boy came by his death, the events following the discovery of his body are considered to be among the most shameful chapters in Lincoln's history. A Jewish resident named Jopin was arrested first. Terrified by threats of torture and death, and before being hanged on Canwick Hill, Jopin's coerced testimony led to a series of purges and executions against Lincoln's Jewish community. The episode even drew Henry III and his queen to Lincoln that October.

Jews House (l) and Jews' Court (r).

(Hugh's body was interred in Lincoln Cathedral, where today the remains of his altar tomb bear a plaque cautioning against the fictions and prejudice involved. The boy's skeleton was unearthed there in 1791 and sketched by the artist Grimm before being replaced.)

According to Sympson's *Lincoln* (1906), a spurious tradition linked the boy's alleged murder to Jews' Court, a building on the slope of Steep Hill with medieval origins, which has been extensively redeveloped and now bears a seventeenth-century appearance.

These were unhappy times for Lincoln's Jewish quarter. The chronicler Holinshed tells us that in 1265 insurgent barons attacked Lincoln's Jews, 'entered their synagogue, and burnt the book of their law'. Tradition says this synagogue was also at Jews' Court, in a front room on the first floor.

This building is today a bookshop and home to the Society for Lincolnshire History and Archaeology. Fittingly, in 1992 its Upper Room was also the location for the modern resumption of worship by the Lincolnshire Jewish Community, after a gap of 700 years.

Immediately south, Jew's House (built 1150–60) boasts an original, beautifully moulded arched doorway, over which projects the buttress shaft of a fireplace and chimney. In 1290 this house belonged to another member of the Jewish community, Belasset of Wallingford, who was hanged for 'clipping the king's coin' (and melting the clippings to make new money). It is now a very fine restaurant.

'Little St Hugh's' shrine in the cathedral.

10. Greyfriars

The Franciscan Grey Friars, named after their heavy grey cloaks, came to Lincoln *c.* 1230 with the blessing of William de Beningworth, sub-dean of the cathedral, although Leland tells us Reginaldus Molendinarius, merchant of Lincoln, founded the 'Grey Frares' here. The citizens of Lincoln were asked by Henry III to give the friars a parcel of Guildhall land between (what is now) Free School Lane and Broadgate; here, between 1237 and *c.* 1280, their chapel-friary was constructed.

The Franciscans were devoted to a life of poverty, and dependent upon charitable donations for their parochial services. These included hearing confessions, although in 1379 they even provided sanctuary for an accused murderer, Robert de Swanlound. In 1535 they introduced fresh water to Greyfriars via water pipes in the public highway leading from a spring near Monks' Abbey. Four years later, however, Henry VIII had the friars expelled, and their 'goodly conduit' was appropriated by the city for the lower town's own water needs.

The friary later passed to a prominent Lincolnshire family, the Monsons. Robert Monson, Recorder of Lincoln, established a 'free school' there in 1568, although from 1612 this co-existed with a 'house of correction', where the unemployed and poor were set to work on 'malt-querns'. On 30 May 1644 sparks from a gunpowder explosion on the Cornhill set many houses ablaze, as well as obliterating the original St Swithin's Church. Providentially, Greyfriars was spared the inferno. (The current St Swithin's Church is a Victorian replacement, built somewhat nearer to Greyfriars than the old version.)

The free school, later the Middle School, ceased in 1900, and the ex-friary next reopened as the City and County Museum in 1907. However, at the time of writing it stands empty.

Greyfriars.

11. Monks' Abbey

Monks Road is named after St Mary Magdalene's Cell, a Benedictine religious house belonging to the Abbey of St Mary at York, which was probably founded some time during the reign of Henry II. Also known as Monks' Abbey, the cell's inhabitants were the Black Monks – so called because they wore tunics, cowls and hoods of black material. In its time, the cell was a small one, with only a prior and two or three monks. These devoted their entire life to prayer and looking after the abbey's lands in Lincoln, avoiding interaction with the town's citizens. Therefore, one wonders what squabble with locals caused a monk at the cell to be violently attacked by 'certain men' in 1312.

The cell was dissolved by Henry VIII. Afterwards Monks' Abbey served as farm buildings before falling into ruination. In 1870 part of the monks' former land – the Monks' Leys – was bought by the City Corporation (forerunner of the City Council) and turned into the Arboretum public park.

The main ruin (three walls of the chapel) dates to the late fourteenth/early fifteenth century, although portions of the remains may date back to the 1200s. The parcel of land immediately north-east (where the playground is) displays traces of the monks' fish or mill pond. The monks utilized a nearby iron-rich spring, later called 'Monks Well', which was still being sought out for its healing properties by the early 1800s.

Monks' Abbey.

12. John of Gaunt's Palace

At one time a mansion stood at the corner of Gaunt Street and High Street, going by the name John of Gaunt's Palace. This building is believed to have originated with a Lincoln merchant family, the Suttons, of whom John Sutton (d. 1391) was Mayor of Lincoln. Sutton was a vassal of John of Gaunt, granted certain lands in return for his homage; therefore, the building had that prince's arms displayed on a shield beneath a gable.

This 'palace' remained almost complete until 1737, and is said to have been very impressive, with fine stone perpendicular windows, buttresses and battlements. In 1849 – the building having been converted into two modern mansions – an exquisite oriel window was removed for safe-keeping and installed in Lincoln Castle's gateway passage. By the mid-twentieth century a garage and showrooms sat on the site, with only fragments and foundations of the original palace still existing.

There is a tradition that the prince had the mansion built himself as a residence for Catherine de Swynford (the poet Chaucer's sister-in-law). Catherine was the widow of a Kettlethorpe knight, and John of Gaunt married her in Lincoln Cathedral in 1396. But her previous love affair with him and the denial of their offspring to the English crown, after having previously been legitimized, has become the stuff of historical romance. She died in 1403 and her tomb lies in Lincoln Cathedral.

The largely fifteenth-century red-brick house on Pottergate, with its beautiful stone oriel window, is today sometimes called 'Catherine Swynford's house', as the original building was her residence between *c.* 1387 and the time of her marriage. Its actual name, however, was The Chancery because before Catherine's time it was the residence (*c.* 1321) of Antony Bek, Chancellor of Lincoln Cathedral. Parts of the house, which is now known as the Deanery, date back to the early twelfth century.

Palace oriel window, now in Lincoln Castle.

Above: Catherine's tomb.

Below: The Chancery, Catherine's former residence.

13. Exchequer Gate

Still protecting the western edge of Minster Yard, or Cathedral Close, is the formidable Exchequer Gate.

Around 1285 Bishop Oliver Sutton first appealed to King Edward I for a 12-foot-high enclosure to ring the precinct, protecting canons and ministers resorting to the cathedral at midnight to say matins. Work on the enclosure only began around thirty years later, it being accepted that there had of late been homicides and other crimes committed in the lanes around the precinct. The wall was finished around 1327, the Exchequer Gate being its western access. Ostensibly built to house the dean and chapter's financial records and registers, the threat of violence accounts for its defensive aspect; on each side of the main arch are elegant octagonal turrets, surmounted with battlements. To obtain some perspective, what we call the Exchequer Gate today was only the *inner* gateway of an enclosed square, for it also had an *outer* gateway.

On 2 July 1643, the Exchequer Gate was the scene of civil war action. Lincoln then being under Parliament, forty Royalist infiltrators hidden in the dean's house tried to seize ammunition from the outer gatehouse, in an attempt to help King Charles I's forces seize Lincoln. They were bombarded with cannon fire and

Exchequer Gate.

several died in the melee. Although a heroic failure, Royalists nonetheless entered Lincoln shortly afterwards and briefly held the city.

Until the 1700s Cathedral Close's gates were locked nightly. The Exchequer Gate's outer gateway was pulled down over 200 years ago, and what is left has been much restored. Today, the central arch has a worn stone tablet in the floor commemorating Lincoln's first Christmas Market (10 December 1982).

Another relic of this encircling wall is the small arched postern, or back, gate near the summit of Greestone Stairs. It was through this unguarded door that in 1726 a mob of 500 surged, protesting about plans to dismantle spires on the cathedral's western towers. The workmen were beaten and driven away, with the disorder ensuring the two spires remained until 1807.

Pottergate Arch protected the southern entrance to the Close. (Incidentally, it was north of this arch, outside 13 Minster Yard, that the carriage of Colonel Coningsby Sibthorp, Lincoln's MP, crashed in February 1821, seriously injuring him. There was speculation the vehicle had been sabotaged, for Lincoln citizens were highly agitated at the time. That July saw rioting against King George IV so violent that the soldiery had to be called in to quell it.) Other portions of what would once have been an imposing defensive ring surrounding the cathedral are observable on Winnowsty Lane and Priory Gate (rebuilt 1816). The stone wall lining Eastgate, with its little ornamental figure glowering accusingly along the street, isn't part of the ring, however; this is a remnant portion of the original Deanery (*c.* 1254 to 1847) and Works Chantry House.

Below left: Greestone Stairs postern gate.

Below right: Pottergate portion of the wall.

Priorygate, rebuilt in 1816. On the left are The Rest and former Elephant Inn (late 1600s).

14. Witch and Wardrobe

This pub on Waterside North dates mainly to the sixteenth century, although portions of it are much older. It is a patchwork of many eras, according to its own information board. The thirteenth century, low door-framed walls of the original core are inside, and from the fifteenth century onwards the building saw enlargements, additions, alterations and restoration work until the twentieth century.

Lodged in the western side is a fifteenth-century tomb, built into the wall. Inside the pub, an oak spiral staircase from the seventeenth century was discovered in the 1970s secreted behind false walls west of the bar. Tradition has it that centuries ago an old woman broke her neck falling down these stairs, which can still be seen; her restless spirit now haunts the pub.

The Witch and Wardrobe (named after CS Lewis' children's story) is two dwellings knocked into one and therefore hasn't always been a pub. In its lifetime it has been a River Witham trading post, and in the late nineteenth century a basket maker's workshop and the Liberal Club until 1890. From 1905 it was the A1 Fish & Oyster Saloon, which became, until 1979, the famous A1 fish and chip shop.

Above: Witch and Wardrobe.

Right: Supposed tomb in west wall.

15. Whitefriars

Hidden away down a tiny alley leading east off High Street is a fifteenth-century timber-framed house called 'Whitefriars'.

The White Friars, or Carmelites, were established in Lincoln *c.* 1269, although their friary was on the *other* side of High Street a significant distance away. It was in the Great Hall of their friary that King Edward II held a parliament in 1316, to organise the Scottish war. However, the friary came down in the 1500s; from 1846, St Mark's railway station sat on the site.

Therefore, 'Whitefriars' original purpose is an enigma. The early Victorian Lincolnshire architect James Sandby Padley, who sketched it, commented, 'There is a tradition that this building anciently formed part of a White Friary.' If so, it was a very late addition to the friary complex. After the Dissolution of the Monasteries it appears to have been converted into several dwellings.

The alleyway 'Whitefriars' hides in is called 'Akrill's Passage' after William Akrill who ran a bakery there in the early 1800s. In 1930 the *Echo* called the building 'the most obscure of Lincoln's antiquities' and today it is still just that: a mysterious centuries-old house that is passed by thousands on High Street daily who barely know of its existence.

Whitefriars, Akrill's Passage.

16. The Cardinal's Hat

At the bottom of the Strait is The Cardinal's Hat. This three-storey, timber-framed town house is of late fifteenth-century origin, and was the home of the Grantham family (hence Grantham Street beside it), who were prominent wool merchants.

The Grantham family cannot be mentioned without reference to an ancient, now gone church, St Martin's, where they were interred in the north aisle of the chancel. This stood in the vicinity of Garmston Street nearby. The tomb of one of them, Sir Thomas Grantham, and his first wife Frances, eventually ended up in St Mary le Wigford. Sir Thomas, who died in 1630, was Lincoln's MP at the time King Charles I dissolved parliament in 1629 – an act that fueled the oncoming civil war.

However, by the time of the war the Cardinal's Hat had long been a tavern, with the Grantham family having relocated in the early 1500s. In the wake of their departure the house was supposedly named after Cardinal Thomas Wolsey – a Bishop of Lincoln in 1514 and afterwards the powerful Archbishop of York and Lord Chancellor, until he fell afoul of Henry VIII.

Both the tavern and nearby St Martin's Church were severely damaged during the conflict. The Cardinal's Hat was luckier than the church, though, which was shattered by Parliamentary cannon in 1644, and only rebuilt in 1740.

Cardinal's Hat.

The church is now completely gone, pulled down in the 1870s, although its tower survived until 1921. Gravestones can be seen in St Martin's Square, evidencing its former graveyard.

The Cardinal's Hat was occupied mid-twentieth century by the St John Ambulance Brigade and restored in 1952–53, although it is presently a modern, vibrant bar. Further along Grantham Street is where the Lincoln Divisional HQ of St John's is now stationed: their stone-framed door has an eye-catching monkey-like carving adorning it.

On the Cardinal's Hat's northern side is another building of similar design: Dernstall House, a late fifteenth-century town house with an open-roofed hall on its first floor. It is named after The Dernstall – Lincoln's medieval Jewish quarter at the south end of the Strait.

17. Lincoln Guildhall and Stonebow

Originally, a guild of Lincoln's leading citizens transacted town business in a 'Guild Hall' between (where is now) Free School Lane and Broadgate, but in 1237 they relocated to a room over the 'Stanbogh'. This was an arched gateway, itself situated on the site of a third-century Roman gatehouse that had once marked the entrance to the lower Roman town.

Here, among other medieval civic business, aldermen sat as a court of justice and heard the pleas of the city. Around 1390 the mayor's bailiffs collected money from reluctant citizens for a replacement building; as the gateway was becoming unfit for purpose. The money appears to have been initially misused however, and the replacement 'Stonebow' didn't actually develop on the site until the late fifteenth century. Over time there has been much alteration either side but the main archway still looks as it did when reconstructed. The upper storey – the Guildhall – was added *c.* 1520. (Remarkably, below ground, ancient medieval cells still exist, with the wall of one such room being formed by a subterranean portion of the even older Roman southern wall.)

On the south front, in slender towers either side of the wide central archway, are statues: of the Archangel Gabriel holding a scroll and of the Virgin Mary above a small serpent. These statues are possibly relics of the original 'Stanbogh'. Between them are the royal arms of King James I; and on either side, the city coat of arms.

The Guildhall's windows were smashed during an election riot in Georgian times. Until 1809 it served as a court of justice, holding the city quarter sessions. The portion east of the arch functioned as a disgusting gaol, described in 1802 by a prison reformer named Neild as 'one of the worst in the kingdom', full of intoxicated, half-starved, half-suffocated prisoners. The eastern section was rebuilt in 1842.

On the roof hangs the Motte Bell, dating from 1371. Today, this still tolls to summon members to their civic business in the Council Chamber over

Stonebow and Guildhall.

the centre arch. With its richly decorated open timber roof and handsome mayor's throne, this hall is almost filled by a long councillor's table. It is said this was installed in the days of duels, being so wide as to prevent attendees stabbing each other across it.

The Guildhall is also the official home of Lincoln's mayor. Those who have held this office from 1206 include Maria Nevile, in 1925 the first female mayor. The mayor in turn chooses the Sheriff of Lincoln, and the first female to hold this office was Emily Gilbert in 1936. Emily was a groundbreaker in other ways: she became Lincoln's first woman motorist in 1899.

Today, the site of the former gaol houses a fine collection of civic insignia, including a ceremonial mace from the reign of Charles I, and a weighty sword presented by King Richard II in 1387 to Mayor John Sutton. Perhaps most remarkable is a royal charter from 1157 confirming the townsfolk's right to a merchant guild and other privileges. This document predates the Magna Carta.

Above: Part of the Guildhall's subterranean medieval gaol.

Left: The Council Chamber.

Right: Sword presented by Richard II.

Below: Lincoln's 1157 charter – older than the Magna Carta.

18. High Bridge/ Stokes

High Bridge was built around 1160. It carries High Street across the River Witham, and is the only bridge from this era in Britain still bearing houses. The timber-framed buildings upon it date to 1540 and make an imposing sight with their upper storeys jettied forward. However, it was not always so. They were given a brick façade in the nineteenth century, and it was not until 1902 that their Tudor charm was carefully revealed under the supervision of Lincoln architect William Watkins. Most of the visible timber is the sixteenth-century original, and during the renovation carvings of King Edward VII and Queen Alexandra were added to the top corners to celebrate their coronation (also in 1902). Since the early 1900s, Stokes' High Bridge Café has been situated within.

There used to be a late twelfth-century chapel on the bridge's eastern side dedicated to St Thomas the Martyr. An obelisk and water conduit replaced the chapel from 1763 until 1939, and in 1996 this was reconstructed in St Mark's shopping precinct using fragments of the original, including its famous pineapple ornament.

Stokes' Coffee House building, dated 1540.

Above left: High Street *c.* 1900. Note the obelisk on High Bridge; the church tower in the background is that of St Peter at Arches, now gone.

Above right: St Mark's obelisk incorporates parts of the one that stood on High Bridge.

Beside Stokes', narrow steps lead down to a passage that follows the Witham to the Brayford Pool. The dark, arched underside of High Bridge, through which the river flows, is at this spot called the Glory Hole. Due to the growing difficulties of waterborne traffic passing beneath it, this historic bridge narrowly avoided being pulled down in 1803.

19. Leigh-Pemberton House

Looming over Castle Hill is the jettied Tudor building called Leigh-Pemberton House. Its east side overlooks the old Roman main street, or *via principalis* (today's Bailgate). Although striking, it is often overlooked because of its position sandwiched between the mighty castle and the majestic cathedral.

Built around 1543 as a city merchant's residence, it is an impressive example – internally and externally – of half-timbered work. Its south front is triple-gabled, and the south-east corner has an original post with carved figure and bracket. In 1929 the building was extensively restored by the National Provincial Bank, and again in 1970 when it was utilized by the National Westminster Bank Ltd. On 31 May 1979 the building was presented to the dean and chapter of Lincoln,

Above: Leigh-Pemberton House.

Left: Original Tudor figure carving on the house.

for the cathedral to use as it saw fit: in recognition of this benefaction, it was named after the bank's then chairman, Robert Leigh-Pemberton, who later became Governor of the Bank of England.

A house of similar development, recorded in 1624 as the Great Garrett, and now the Green Dragon, looks out over Thorngate in the lower town.

2c. Lion and Snake

The Lion and Snake in Bailgate has a claim to be the oldest pub in Lincoln. Tradition states that it originated in the fifteenth century, and has served no other function than that of a tavern since. The pub as seen today is believed to have developed from two separate tenements; but whatever the case, it was at various times the Ram Inn, the Red Lyon, the Earl of Scarborough's Arms, and The Red Lyon and Snake. It seems to date to at least 1549 because that year there is a record of the leasing 'of a tenement in the Bail called the Ramme'.

In the 1740s the inn was the scene of betting on cockfights, 'two guineas a battle'. The inn is also mentioned during a report into Lincoln's dire state of sanitation in 1848, when a well in its yard was described as so obnoxious it had killed a woman merely passing by who breathed in its fumes too deeply. Until around the 1860s it was a popular venue for auctions, where properties and parcels of land were bid for.

Lion and Snake.

21. Quaker Meeting House

Nestled on Beaumont Fee is the Meeting House of the Religious Society of Friends, or Quakers.

The building is in an area formerly called the Manor of Hungate – a post-Norman private estate with its own court, ruled by a succession of lords of the manor. It was exempt from the city's jurisdiction, and under the medieval Beaumonts, the manor became known as 'The Liberty of Beaumont Fee', 'fee' meaning a parcel of land. The Beaumonts lost the estate during the Wars of the Roses.

The manor had its own church, St Mary Crackpole's. This church – named after a pool frequented by crows – disappeared *c.* 1549 and the parish merged with that of St Martin's on Garmston Street. St Mary Crackpole's graveyard thereafter became an overspill for St Martin's – and in time shrank to the portion now observable on Beaumont Fee.

On the southwestern edge of this graveyard the Society of Friends Meeting House was built *c.* 1689. The Quakers were a dissenting Christian religious movement that emerged during the civil wars, and they had previously visited Lincolnshire. In 1654 an early Quaker missionary, John Whitehead, had been assaulted and nearly murdered by a mob in front of the cathedral before soldiers intervened; other Quaker converts died in Lincoln in 1657 and 1658 after being imprisoned for non-payment of tithes.

Nonetheless, the 'Friends' persevered. They even had their own small graveyard plot on the building's north side. Today, the Meeting Hall still serves the same purpose as it did in the 1680s.

Religious democracy was absent in those days: in 1688 a small Catholic chapel and school in the Bail were torn down by a mob supporting the Glorious Revolution. On Monson Street, however, the Unitarian Chapel (1725) still functions – a second surviving example of an old building historically used for 'dissenting' worship in Lincoln.

Quaker Meeting House.

22. Christ's Hospital Bluecoat School

Lincoln's Christ's Hospital Bluecoat School was founded by Dr Richard Smith, who died at Welton in 1602 and left money for a charitable school institution in Lincoln. After several years' delay a permanent Bluecoat School was established at the summit of Steep Hill, in St Michael's churchyard. Here, twelve poor boys were clothed, educated and maintained until they were eligible for apprenticeships. (The term 'Bluecoat' derived from the long blue cassocks they wore.) The school flourished and the number of boys was greatly increased. A new larger building replaced it in 1784, with a tympanum legend referencing its origins: *Founded by Richard Smith MD June 1st 1612*.

The school closed in 1883, on the basis that by that time elementary education was adequately provided for elsewhere in the city. However, the building's connections with education are not lost, for it is now used by the University of Lincoln.

The Lincoln Girls' School on Lindum Hill was one of the new schools established using endowments from the Christ's Hospital Foundation following the Bluecoat School's dissolution. An 1893 cornerstone commemorates the Girls'

Below left: Site of the former Bluecoat School, the door on the right bearing an inscription to Smith.

Below right: Stained glass at Welton, showing Blue Coat boys marching under the Stonebow on 21 December, following an annual tradition.

Endowments from the Bluecoat School established the Girls' School.

School's link to Christ's, and above the door on the Greestone side is the motto *Disce aut discede* – 'Learn or Get Out'. There were several fatalities here during the Second World War when an RAF bomber plunged into the school's Boarding House (now demolished). More recently, this glorious terracotta-bricked facility, which may be said to owe its existence partly to the Bluecoat school, has become Lincoln University Technical College.

23. White Hart Hotel

The prestigious White Hart Hotel is a Georgian addition to upper Lincoln, dating to at least the 1760s. Tradition states, however, that the original 'White Hart' on this spot was a coaching inn, established to commemorate the visit to Lincoln in 1387 of King Richard II. On this occasion, Richard granted Lincoln's mayor the right to have a sword borne before him on civic occasions. The White Hart was the king's emblem, 'hart' being an archaic word for 'stag'. Today, a white stag statue surmounting a clock looks out over the building's Eastgate corner.

As well as luxury bedrooms, the hotel has a meeting room called the Tank Room. This is so named because William Tritton and Major Walter Wilson conceived the design there in September 1915 for a war engine capable of crossing a 5-foot trench. Sketches by Tritton's draughtsman, William Rigby, of unworkable designs for what became the 'tank' were burned in the room's fire there and then, due to the secrecy required.

The White Hart used to display a large ornamental stag over its main entrance as well.

Tritton Road, leading out of the city, is named after Sir William, who was knighted in 1917. His nearby agricultural engineering company, William Foster & Co., a 25-acre site between Firth Road and Waterloo Street, manufactured and trialed the first fighting tanks. The prototype 'Little Willie' and its successor 'Mother' ultimately helped end the First World War's stalemate of trench warfare.

24. Assembly Rooms

The Assembly Rooms in Bailgate were built by public subscription for county functions. Opened to the public in 1745, it is a building illustrative of a reinvigorated city, coinciding with the redevelopment of trade along the Fossdyke Canal.

Above: Assembly Rooms, uphill.

Left: The Butter Market façade was relocated from Silver Street to Waterside South in 1938. 'Downhill's' Assembly Rooms had been upstairs.

The building's ballroom was 70 feet by 30 feet, and from 1789 was the setting for an annual Stuff Ball – 'stuff' being the long wool of which Lincolnshire was a staple producer. A century later, the Lincolnshire historian William White observed the ball was still held, although ladies were no longer expected to dance in uncomfortable 'stuff dresses'.

In 1790 it was ransacked by intruders, and in 1815 a swindler fled with a small fortune after advertising a false concert there. Many attended a Masonic Ball in 1858, and at various times between 1890 and 2013 it was a Masonic Temple. The Bailgate entrance and foyer were added in 1914.

An element of snobbery discouraged people from 'downhill' Lincoln being admitted, so in 1757 City Assembly Rooms were established above the Butter Market, which stood approximately at the junction of Silver Street and High Street next to a now gone church, St Peter-at-Arches. Both were taken down in the 1930s, although the Butter Market's façade was carefully recreated in 1938 and incorporated into the Central Market, Waterside South.

25. Smith, Ellison & Brown

Lincoln's first bank, Smith, Ellison & Brown, was established in 1775. Abel Smith of Nottingham was one of England's most eminent bankers, while John Brown was a local textile merchant and former mayor. Yorkshire-born Richard Ellison had made a fortune from tolls he charged, the City Corporation in 1741 having leased the Fossdyke navigation to him for 999 years.

Their small bank sat just north of the Stonebow, being run from Brown's home. Early ledgers reveal the purchase of saddlebags in 1776 for fetching coins, and of two pistols for protection against highwaymen.

Smith died in 1788, Ellison and Brown in 1792. Thereafter, the bank was run by descendants of Smith and Ellison.

Whereas Ellison had helped revolutionise trade on the Fossdyke waterway by financing essential modernisation, expansion and maintenance, his successors neglected this. A later Ellison continued to collect the revenues from the Fossdyke tolls, while paying the City Corporation their annuity; but because his bank controlled the Corporation's finances at every level they were powerless to get him to improve the waterway. The Ellison family withdrew in 1859, having previously sold the Fossdyke lease to the railways.

The original bank was much nearer the Stonebow, crowding in on the west side of the arch; however, it was rebuilt (and set back) in the 1880s, in a Renaissance palazzo style. The bank later merged with the Union Bank of London Ltd. and is now home to NatWest Lincoln Smiths Bank.

The bank's location was appropriate. The names of nearby Mint Street, Mint Lane and Silver Street indicate that coins were historically minted hereabouts, from the Danish era until perhaps the thirteenth century.

Above left: NatWest building (1880s), on the site of the former Smith, Ellison & Co.

Above right: Brass plaques are evidence of its former incarnations.

26. Ellis' Mill

Ellis' Mill on Mill Road is the sole survivor of nine windmills which once proudly lined the vantage ground of Burton Ridge. It dates to 1798, replacing a mid-seventeenth-century forerunner, and saw a succession of owners until it became the property of John Ellis *c.* 1892 after his previous windmill on the ridge – the Burton Mill – fell down. Still going strong in 1931, when it ground barley for pig-meal, the mill ceased operating in the 1940s. In 1974 – a year after Ellis' family relinquished their ownership of the now derelict building – it suffered a devastating fire.

A restoration project began under the Lincoln Civic Trust in 1977, using parts either cannibalized from other county windmills or purpose-built, and in 1981 the first flour was ground there in forty years. During the work a mysterious hoard of early twentieth-century coins was discovered in a soldered tin that had

Ellis' Mill.

been cemented into the wall with a bank slip dated 1951. The mill is currently closed 'due to health and safety concerns'. Nonetheless, it continues to provide a captivating reminder of a local trade that four generations or so back would have been taken for granted.

27. Theatre Royal

There has been a playhouse in Lincoln since at least 1744, when one opened in a lane under the castle (later Drury Lane) for William Herbert's Company of Comedians. Nearby, the late fifteenth-century half-timbered building atop Steep Hill became an actors' tavern, the Harlequin, before the theatrical circuit migrated downhill in 1763 to a building in the King's Arms Yard, Clasketgate. In 1806 a replacement brick-built theatre opened, which included a musician's pit, two rows of boxes and one gallery supported by iron columns.

On the morning of 27 November 1892, this playhouse – by now christened the Theatre Royal – was engulfed by fire. Firemen using water from the street

Left: Theatre Royal (1893).

Below: Former actors' tavern (currently unoccupied).

mains battled the inferno, watched by a huge crowd, but the building was utterly destroyed when an explosion brought the roof down.

The rebuilt Theatre Royal opened in December 1893, with a production of *Charley's Aunt*, a comedy in three acts. This was the theatre's fourth incarnation, and it provided good views unobstructed by pillars, which had been a problem with the previous version.

Lately, the venue has been relaunched as the New Theatre Royal. Incidentally, the Theatre Royal was among the first venues in Lincoln to screen early films, or 'pictures'. On 30 June 1913 it even screened an early colour film, made using a process called 'Kinemacolor'.

28. The Lawn

The Greek Revival-style Lincoln Lunatic Asylum (later the Lawn Hospital) opened on 8 November 1820 west of the castle. Designed by Richard Ingleman, it was purpose-built, with male and female wings, and a dramatic central portico dominating the south front. In 1827 a number of new wards and other accommodations were made for the classification of patients, separating them according to their circumstances, and offering outdoor open spaces, exercise and employment: 'the cornerstone of complete recovery'. The facility's boundary walls were even built out of sight, below the hill's brow, so patients would not feel imprisoned.

The Lawn – a former asylum.

Vice-President and physician Edward Charlesworth MD, among others, strove to treat patients in a more enlightened manner, dispensing with the straightjackets and shackles used as standard at the time. Under house-surgeon Robert Gardiner Hill, medical restraining was practically abolished by the 1830s. Their challenge in changing attitudes can be appreciated by an 1841 report, which reveals that, even in a progressive hospital like this one, allegations of violent discipline by nurses and keepers were frequent.

Notwithstanding a duel he fought near the racecourse in 1824, when he and Colonel Charles Sibthorpe fired at each other and missed, Charlesworth's contribution to health care in England was immense. There is a statue of him in the south-east corner of the grounds.

The Lawn was bought by the City Council in 1985, who in 2014 sold it to Stokes' as a coffee-roasting house. It has some interesting neighbours. Hilton House, home of the celebrated landscape painter Peter de Wint (d. 1849), together with its striking blue Italianate lodge, stands opposite on Union Road. The now demolished Lincoln Union Workhouse, built in 1837, was also hereabouts, its walled entrance surviving between 8 and 10 Burton Road. In its time, this complex exceeded even The Lawn in size.

Edward Charlesworth's statue.

29. Strugglers Inn, Westgate

Of executions, we learn of a one-off death sentence being carried out on the South Common in 1741. This was of a grenadier, Robert Bonner, shot for desertion. But until 1814 all other criminals were publicly hanged at the junction of Burton Road and Westgate. Occasionally, women were publicly burned at a stake near the gallows if convicted of murdering their husbands.

Multiple executions were not unknown. On 18 March 1785 there occurred the largest mass hanging in living memory, of nine prisoners, while four died on the gallows in 1810. In 1789, the crowd watched robber George Kilpike – sometime *after* being hanged – lift up his right hand and place it in his waistcoat, before it was confirmed he had finally expired.

By the time the 'Struggler beer-shop' opened opposite this site *c.* 1830, public executions had moved to the castle's Cobb Hall roof. On 11 April 1836 the Struggler's owner exposed the original second-century Roman West Gate, buried in the castle's ramparts, when he extended his garden. The gate was reburied, although it had partly collapsed, and the landlord was gaoled for compromising one of his majesty's fortifications should war come to England.

In 1877 a poacher, William Clarke, was hanged inside the castle (after the cessation of public executions) for fatally shooting a gamekeeper at Norton Disney. The Struggler beerhouse's then landlord, William Roberts, who ran the

Above: Clarke's lurcher.

Right: Strugglers Inn.

pub until 1890, adopted Clarke's lurcher. However, the dog pined to death and Roberts afterwards had it stuffed and mounted behind the bar, where it became a frequent topic of conversation. In the 1980s this unique curiosity was given to the castle, where it can now be seen. Clarke's pitiful headstone can also be seen in the castle's Lucy Tower graveyard.

Subsequently, executions of murderers took place inside Greetwell Road's prison.

30. Boultham Hall

The Ellison family acquired the Boultham estate, west of the Witham, in 1827. For generations the new Boultham Hall saw Ellison weddings, births, family bereavements and summer entertainments, but in the early days there was also drama. In 1833, an Ellison servant of forty years shot himself in a dispute over a reference, while in 1839 Lt Col Richard Ellison stabbed and seriously wounded a man named Seely on the Witham banks, apparently after mistaking him for a poacher. Poaching was a recurring problem: in 1857, a member of the Ellison family battled two armed poachers in a potato field near the hall.

William White's gazetteer of Lincolnshire described the hall in 1872 as 'a handsome mansion, in a finely wooded park (which) has been much enlarged and improved by Colonel Ellison, and is now occupied by his son, Major R.G. Ellison'. Two years later it was thrown open for galas, garden parties and fetes. (This author's own great-grandmother, Nellie Brumpton, would often speak of the picnics held annually on the Boultham estate during the first years of the twentieth century, when little girls from a local Sunday school, of which she was one, attended dressed in their best pinafores.)

The hall became vacant in 1909. Sold in 1913 by R. G. Ellison's son, it next functioned as an Auxiliary Hospital during the First World War. Since 1929 the estate has been a public park.

Boultham Hall was pulled down in 1959, although echoes of its grandeur remain. The hall's footprint is now a park feature, while ex-lodges grace the estate's former entrances on Hall Drive (north) and Boultham Park Road (west). The latter entry has ornamented piers dating to 1872, which were fitted in the 1930s with gates taken from Monk's Manor, Joseph Ruston's former estate off Greetwell Road. Perhaps least recognised is a former gatehouse, between Dixon and Peel Streets. Bearing the Ellison crest of a griffin's head and dated 1883, this led off High Street onto a long private driveway, traversing what was then rural scenery to connect with the estate at Boultham Park Road.

In Boultham's St Helen's churchyard there is a huge granite block, which formed part of the Sebastopol fortifications. This was brought back to Lincoln by Major R. G. Ellison and placed there in memory of the men belonging to his regiment (the 47th) who fell in the Crimean War.

Above: Boultham Hall *c.* 1901.

Below: Ellison memorials and the Sebastopol boulder.

31. Sessions House

Reporting on the Sessions House, *The History of Lincoln* (1816) noted: 'The City Jail and Sessions House is situated on the New Road (Lindum Hill), and has more the appearance of a gentleman's house than a prison. The first stone for this building was laid in 1805, by Robert Fowler, mayor, and it was finished in 1809, during the mayoralty of Thomas Colton, who held the first sessions there on the 15th of July. The assizes were also held on the same day, by Judge Heath.' During these hearings Heath sentenced a prisoner, Joseph Ranworth, to death for burglary, although he was later reprieved.

The gaol and Sessions House were rebuilt in 1844, on an improved model so as to admit by classification of offenders. This was after complaints by reformers that, like the Stonebow before it, it was completely unfit for purpose, with prisoners of all types, convicted or otherwise, thrown in together. A police station was also incorporated as part of the Session House's modernisation. Until 1940 the premises were guarded by an old Crimean War cannon.

In 1870 the gaol held 206 prisoners, but by 1878 all inmates had been transferred to the new HMP Lincoln on Greetwell Road. By the 1970s it was apparent that the Session House's courthouse was once more unfit for purpose. The police station part having relocated to the jokingly named 'Ryvita House' on West Parade, in 1990 the courthouse was rendered obsolete by the new Lincoln Magistrates' Court on High Street. (This, broadly speaking, today hears 'lower end' crimes and civil matters; indictable offences, such as murder, violent robbery and fraud, progress to the castle's Crown Court.)

The Sessions House is now part of Lincoln College.

Part of the former Sessions House.

32. Lincoln Central Railway Station

Lincoln was among the last big towns to be brought into the railway network, and when it was, two stations came along almost simultaneously. The first, St Mark's, was opened by the Midland Railway Company in 1846 with much fanfare. This was the Nottingham to Lincoln line.

The Great Northern Railway's Peterborough to Lincoln line followed, establishing Lincoln Central station in 1848, which was built in the Tudor Revival style with a crenellated tower.

Both stations' lines crossed the High Street at different points a mere 500 feet apart – an inconvenience that caused infuriation and congestion for generations. In the twentieth century there was a long-standing joke that when this was introduced all robberies in Lincoln ceased. This was because the two sets of barriers halted High Street traffic so regularly that it made any escape by thieves utterly impossible.

In the small hours of 3 June 1962, the 'Night Scotsman' – a sleeper train from King's Cross to Edinburgh – catastrophically derailed just east of Lincoln Central near Pelham Bridge. Three people died and seven were injured when multiple carriages were thrown onto their sides.

St Mark's closed in 1985, being transformed into a shopping precinct, and all services were concentrated via one line on Lincoln Central station. A Midland Railway tablet commemorating eleven St Mark's workers killed in the First World War was relocated to Lincoln Central at the time.

In 2008, £55 million was spent on modernising Lincoln Central. Ten years later it also benefitted from a £30 million 'transport hub' project, gaining a pedestrianized plaza on St Mary's Street that connected it with the new Lincoln Central Bus Station and Car Park.

Portico of former St Mark's railway station.

Lincoln Central station.

33. Ruston Buildings, Waterside South

The coming of industry catapulted Lincoln into the modern era. Among other visionaries, Nathaniel Clayton and Joseph Shuttleworth went into partnership and established the Stamp End Iron Works, while Robey & Co. trialed a traction engine on Canwick Hill in 1860. From the 1840s Lincoln began to change from a busy market town into an industrial hub, expanding rapidly to become an important centre for the production of agricultural machinery and steam engines.

Today, the casual observer can see vivid echoes of Lincoln's industrial heritage on Waterside South. The fancy façade of Doughty's Oil Mill, dated 1863,

Waterside South, site of Ruston, Proctor & Co. in the 1850s before this expanded rapidly; further along, former Doughty's Oil Mill.

appears eye-catchingly out of place, while further along stands part of an Edwardian-era Clayton & Shuttleworth building, with the latter's name emblazoned clearly. Elsewhere, former Robey & Co. Ltd buildings sit along Canwick Road, the main entrance (surmounted by a globe) still plainly visible; while St Swithin's Church displays on its Broadgate side a large, inscribed stone announcing it was placed there by Nathaniel Clayton, of East Cliff House, in 1879.

Gigantic engineering plants developed, employing thousands of workers and becoming places of apprenticeship for generations, while their founders became household names citywide. Among these pioneers, the name of Joseph Ruston, a Justice of the Peace, mayor, politician and philanthropist, is perhaps most familiar. His name has been indelibly stamped on Lincoln engineering since 1857 when he joined Messrs Burton and Proctor's small millwright's business on Waterside South. This expanded as the Sheaf Iron Works, with Ruston eventually becoming sole proprietor and chairman. By the time of his death in 1897 his works had become a gargantuan industrial complex covering 17 acres and employing 2,550 people.

Over time Ruston's underwent a number of transformations. During the First World War, the company turned to building submarine engines, boilers, torpedo parts, gun fittings and appliances for minesweeping and submarine capture. By 1918 it was Ruston and Hornsby Ltd, later becoming Ruston Gas Turbines in the 1960s, and finally a subsidiary of Siemens.

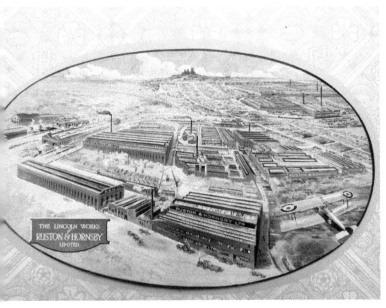

Above: Industrial Lincoln from *Our Part in the Great War* (1919). Note the former Ruston's Coulson Road factory on the left, where aircraft engines were made.

Right: Joseph Ruston's grave, Eastgate.

Ruston's name, faded above a bricked-up entrance to Ruston and Hornsby's Dining Hall on Waterside South .

34. Le Tall's Crown Mill

Towering over Princess Street is the former Le Tall's Crown Mill. The windmill was constructed in the mid-1800s and at one time had six almighty sails. It was purchased by Messrs Henry le Tall Ltd of Woodhouse in 1871. He began to revolutionize its flour-making productivity in the 1880s, fashioning it on an elaborate scale with modern appliances and a steam-powered roller system. Warehouses and a silo were later incorporated. Le Tall died in 1913 and this glorious structure today comprises occupied residential flats.

Princess Street was the scene of a tragedy in 1911. Unrest linked to a national railway strike had beset Lincoln, spiraling out of control into several nights of vandalism, looting, arson and violent clashes with police. Great numbers were injured and the uprising only petered out when soldiers were brought into the city. On 23 August Osborne's motorcycle works on Princess Street was set alight, and two men – fireman/PC Alfred Clay and a High Street picture-framer named Starmer – were killed when a wall at the premises collapsed onto them as they assessed the damage, while being mobbed by an aggressive crowd. Initially, it had been thought that it was le Tall's mill that was on fire.

Above: The former mill is now private apartments.

Right: Clay's grave in St Swithin's Cemetery.

35. HMP Lincoln, Greetwell Road

Her Majesty's Prison Lincoln was built in 1869–72, on the open grid system and with a castellated gateway. Initially it housed both sexes, but by the early twentieth century women were incarcerated at Nottingham instead. It also became the only prison for almost all the county.

It was from this Gothic fortress that Irish republican leader Éamon de Valera (incarcerated for a so-called 'German plot') and two others escaped. De Valera managed to steal the key to the exercise yard's gate from the chaplain, make an impression of it in wax and smuggle its dimensions to supporters outside. A replica key was subsequently smuggled back into the prison in a cake and fashioned into a master for all doors. On the night of 3 February 1919, two women brought from Dublin distracted the guards, barbed wire surrounding the prison was cut apart and the rear gate was unlocked using the replica key. Outside, top-ranking republicans, including Michael Collins, assisted de Valera's escape, organising a taxi to collect the group at the eighteenth-century Adam and Eve pub, near Pottergate arch. This, at least, is one version; in October 1950 de Valera, by then a renowned Irish statesman, revisited his old cell at Lincoln gaol and stated, 'The story of my escape has been told very many ways.'

After executions ceased at the castle in 1877, the prison became the place where Lincolnshire's, and later Nottinghamshire's, murderers were hanged. A black flag always flew over the clock tower (behind the gateway) following a hanging.

Pre-empted by the prison bell tolling, the first execution was that of an East Ferry wife murderer named Anderson in 1883. On the morning of his hanging by Lincolnshire hangman William Marwood, Anderson stated miserably, 'There's nothing here I care for.' He was buried within the precincts of the prison, as became usual. The last execution carried out at HMP Lincoln was that of

HMP Lincoln.

Wasyl Gynpiuk, a Polish-Ukrainian convicted of robbing, strangling, decapitating and burying a sixty-three-year-old widow, Louisa Surgey, in Worksop. He was hanged on 27 January 1961.

In 2002 there was a violent eight-hour mutiny at HMP Lincoln, during which one prisoner died, fires were started, and the facility was completely overrun. £2.75 million worth of destruction was caused.

36. Bracebridge Hall

Bracebridge Hall sat near the junction of Newark Road and Brant Road, on the site of a medieval village. It was begun around 1874 for Francis Jonathan Clarke JP, four-time Mayor of Lincoln and prominent Roman Catholic. Clarke had purchased the estate *c.* 1869, and his hall replaced an earlier, smaller building that seems to have existed there since at least 1851. The architect was Lincoln's Albert Vicars, and the new hall was completed in 1883 with an octagonal tower and private chapel. The extravagant entrance hall contained a painted frieze depicting scenes from *The Merry Wives of Windsor* and a floor of coloured marble.

Bracebridge Hall (renamed Grosvenor Hall).

The jolly-looking hall lodge (today a private residence).

Clarke was Lincoln-born, and from the age of nineteen ran a chemist – first on Newland and then on High Street, earning his fortune from a patented 'Blood Mixture' tonic he sold. He died in Bournemouth in 1888, aged forty-six, following a prolonged illness. His body was repatriated to Bracebridge, before being interred in a vault at Bracebridge cemetery. His funeral brought Lincoln to a standstill, and occurred on a bitterly cold day. It seems appropriate that today Bracebridge Hall is a care home, renamed Grosvenor Hall.

The colourful, ornamental brick and timber building with the steeply pitched roofs and tall chimneys at the nearby Brant Road junction was the hall's lodge.

37. Co-operative Building, Free School Lane

The Lincoln Equitable Co-operative Industrial Society began life in 1861 when Gainsborough joiner Thomas Parker and like-minded others formed a committee and set up a store at 1 Napoleon Place, Lincoln. This community retailer began

Above left: Building in Free School Lane displaying the Co-operative name in upper brickwork.

Above right: Co-operative beehive emblem over the door.

trading that September, the aim being to offer a fairer deal to working people by distributing a share of the profits to members via a dividend scheme. Its dual mottos were 'Union is Strength' and the slightly odd (by today's standards) 'Slow but Sure'.

The Napoleon Place building quickly grew too small for purpose, with the Society moving to Waterside South near High Bridge, then Silver Street in 1874, from where magnificent Central Stores premises developed and spread along Free School Lane. This was effectively a gigantic early department store.

In the 1950s Napoleon Place made way for Pelham Bridge, and Thomas Parker House now sits where the Central Stores were. However, part of the latter complex (added in 1888–89) still survives on Free School Lane, displaying a doorway with the Co-op's traditional beehive emblem. Above is the motto *Crescit Paulatim* (Gradually Increases).

Other buildings around Lincoln display motifs showing they were formerly branches of the Co-operative family, including an odd-looking example with a porthole-style attic window on Gresham Street, from 1907. The former sub-central branch at Tanner's Lane, built in the 1890s to cater for a developing High Street, boasts a huge beehive emblem. Some, like the handsome example on Burton Road, built in 1901, or the 1912 building on the corner of High Street and Tealby Street, are still Co-op outlets today.

38. Lincoln County Hospital

The first County Hospital – for the maimed, the sick and the blind – opened in leased accommodation in St Swithin's parish in 1769. This transferred to a purpose-built hospital on Drury Lane in 1777. (This building would later become Lincoln Theological College, and today is named after theology graduate Chad Varah, founder of the Samaritans.)

After a century, a new County Hospital opened on Sewell Road in 1878; its location was in keeping, given that nearby there had since 1847 been a range of fourteen charitable bede-houses complete with their own chapel and burial ground.

On the evening before the August 1942 Bank Holiday a German bomber damaged the hospital's Nurse's Home, a 1914 addition situated nearer Greetwell Road. In 1948 the hospital was transferred to the National Health Service and has continued to expand eastwards along Greetwell Road. Today, it is the largest hospital complex in Lincolnshire.

An interesting feature now sits in the main car park off Greetwell Road: the Caritas statue, which is charity represented by a motherly lady embracing several children. This was presented to the hospital in 1892 by Joseph Ruston, the famous industrialist and Mayor of Lincoln.

Original hospital entrance, near the 1876 foundation stone. The door's inscription says 'Blessed is the man that provideth for the sick and needy'.

County Hospital's Caritas statue.

One of Lincoln's earliest primitive hospitals stood on Wragby Road, opposite Curle Avenue. This was the Hospital of St Giles, belonging to the Augustinian Order. First mentioned in 1280, its ruins were long a feature of the road and the remaining portion was only demolished in 1927. An ancient stone effigy of St Giles, found at the site, is now in the cathedral's Morning Chapel.

39. Liberal Club

The Liberal Club, St Swithin's Square, was opened in March 1892 by Miss Crossfield, the daughter of Lincoln's Liberal political candidate, using a silver key.

The Liberal Club's design of red brick with stone dressings was imposing and confident; it was essentially a men's private club, complete with reading room, billiards room, cards rooms, lecture hall, cooking kitchen, etc. The architects were Sington and Brameld of Manchester, with later rear additions by W. Mortimer and Son.

On 3 December 1910, following a disorderly general election, Winston Churchill, then Liberal Party Home Secretary, broke with convention to make a

Above: The Liberal Club came first…

Below: followed by the Constitutional Club.

polling day speech in Lincoln. This he attempted that afternoon from the Liberal Club's balcony in front of a surging, agitated crowd, who launched volleys of missiles at him. Churchill reportedly yelled, 'Keep your places! Somebody will be killed!' In scenes of riot and violence, he had to be escorted from the club's rear by police. (Evidently, Lincoln could still disgrace itself, even in these times. On 8 October 1908, for instance, ten suffragettes braved an aggressive, missile-pelting crowd on the Cornhill, while campaigning for women to have the vote.)

In 1895 the foundation stone was laid for the rival Constitutional Club on the corner of Broadgate and Silver Street. How best to utilise both these buildings in the modern age at present remains uncertain, however.

40. Sincil Bank Football Stadium

Lincoln City Football Club was officially formed as an amateur association in 1884, although there had been a team playing since the 1860s. After previously using the 'John o Gaunt's football field', Sincil Bank Football Stadium became the club's home in 1895, the players having become a professional Second Division team not long before. The stadium is named after Sincil Dyke, a drainage channel of possibly Roman origin that runs past it. Basic at first, inside ten years the stadium had begun to develop into the forerunner of what we see today.

The stadium now holds over 10,000 people, the largest stand – the Co-op Stand – being visible in all its glory from as far away as the South Common. The north Stacey-West Stand is named after two LCFC supporters who died in the 1985 Bradford City Stadium disaster, during a Lincoln-Bradford match.

Sincil Bank, legendary home of the Imps.

The team's mascot is Poacher the Imp, an amalgamation of a folk song called 'The Lincolnshire Poacher' and the cathedral's famous gargoyle. In 2017 'the Imps' were propelled to national glory when under Danny Cowley they became the first non-league side in 103 years to reach the FA Cup quarter-finals.

Lincoln also has a long history of women's football, going back to the First World War when female employees at the engineering works formed teams like the Ruston Aircraft Girls and the Robey Girls. On 24 March 1917, for example, a charity match was held at Sincil Bank between female teams of munitions workers from Lincoln and Derby; the Lincoln Munition Girls' team won against a much more experienced opponent. This was the genesis of Lincoln Ladies FC, which has lately been controversially rebranded as Notts County Ladies. In 2019, Nettleham Ladies FC was rebranded as Lincoln City Women.

Sincil Bank has been used as a venue for other events. In June 1958 the stands were filled with thousands of schoolchildren for a visit by Queen Elizabeth II and the Duke of Edinburgh – who drove round the ground in an open car, but beneath umbrellas due to the pouring rain. This was prior to the royal couple officially opening Pelham Bridge.

41. Racecourse Grandstand

The racecourse on the Carholme (West Common) was established in 1773. Initially, its horse races attracted spectators of all sorts, not all of them desirable. In 1831, for instance, there were violent clashes between '500 thimble-riggers and gamblers', gentlemen and fox-hunting famers.

The Grandstand for spectators was built in 1897, to commemorate Queen Victoria's diamond jubilee: another building courtesy of architect W. Mortimer & Son. Other stands, including an 1826 original, complemented it at one time, but are now long dismantled.

Grandstand.

Racecourse, near the end of the 'straight mile'.

The stadium-like, terraced Grandstand remains a striking relic of the days when horse racing was a phenomenally popular fixture in Lincoln's sporting and social calendar. The Lincolnshire Handicap was established in 1849. This became the first 'Classic' event of the flat racing (or speed racing without jumps) season, and the 'straight mile' still survives. One who attended post-war events tells me the race began at Bishop Bridge, followed the straight mile, circled the West Common anti-clockwise and crossed the finishing line in front of the Grandstand. (Bark was used to cover Long Leys Road to protect the horses' hooves at that early point in the race.)

The Lincolnshire Handicap ceased to be held in Lincoln after March 1964. The Grandstand later became a community centre. Local Muslims held Friday prayers there for fifteen years, until the grand opening in 2018 of Lincoln's first purpose-built mosque, Lincoln Central Mosque & Cultural Centre, on the site of the former Boultham Park Dairy.

42. Pyewipe Junction

Two miles west of Lincoln Central station there used to be a junction that diverted the rail line to Skellingthorpe. This was Pyewipe Junction, named after the famous Pyewipe Inn on the opposite northern side of the Fossdyke Canal. Established in the late Victorian era, Pyewipe Junction was in its time an integral part of Lincoln's rail network, from 1882 also being the junction for an 'avoiding line' towards Nottinghamshire. Apart from this, it was the site of a large and busy motive power depot, where locomotives were stabled in an engine shed for maintenance and repairs when not in use.

In the late 1960s the junction became inoperative, with the railway complex there vastly simplified to continue serving only as an avoiding line. Over the years the line

Above: Boultham Mere, where this relic is located, is accessed from Tritton Road.

Below: Swanpool, Lincoln's emptiest, most rural part.

to Skellingthorpe came up (becoming replaced by a cycling route) and the Pyewipe Junction's turntable, engine shed, junction box and other buildings came down.

This is with the exception of a single building – Pyewipe Junction's train crew relief cabin and mess room, which still stands covered in graffiti just south of the avoiding line. The building is on the western edge of Boultham Mere Nature Reserve, a former ballast pit connected with the junction's development.

More importantly, the relief cabin sits on the northern extremity of an expanse called Swanpool, named after a (shrinking) pond at its heart, which is surrounded by open fields. Within the city boundary, this is Lincoln's emptiest, most rural space – and therefore dangerously vulnerable to developers.

43. Water Tower

Looming over Westgate is the 105-foot-high Water Tower, a building borne out of the necessity for pure water following the 1904/05 typhoid epidemic that claimed over a hundred lives, and made 1,000 sick. At the time, water was sourced chiefly from the River Witham and its tributaries, and various dykes, ditches and springs. The tower was designed to accept water into its 330,000-gallon capacity inner storage tank via a 22-mile-long pipe from Elkesley. On 4 October 1911 the new supply of fresh water was activated during a ceremony in the Arboretum park, during which a jet of clean water arced 70 feet in the air from a fountain, accompanied by city-wide celebrations, which included a day off from school for children.

The Water Tower is often assumed to be older than it is. This was the intention of the architect, Sir Reginald Blomfield, who designed it with its historical surroundings in mind. The Westgate side displays Lincoln's coat of arms, and all sides have inlay panels containing *fleur-de-lys* – the symbol of the Virgin Mary, to whom the cathedral is dedicated.

Water Tower, from the castle.

44. Usher Gallery

An addition to Lincoln's cultural quarter arrived in 1927, in the form of the Usher Gallery on Lindum Hill. The gallery was the brainchild of James Ward Usher, a Lincoln-born businessman and collector who had inherited a High Street jewelers and watchmakers. He is credited with popularising the Lincoln Imp myth, as an aide to selling jewelry bearing its likeness. Before he died in 1921, Usher bequeathed his priceless art collection to the City Corporation, as well as £60,000 towards the building of an art gallery for display purposes. The classically inspired Usher Gallery was designed by Sir Reginald Blomfield and was ceremonially opened using a gold key by HRH the Prince of Wales. The prince is said to have keenly inspected a portrait of *himself*, lent by the Manchester Gallery.

The site that the gallery came to occupy was fortified during Roman times, and later home to two (now nonexistent) medieval churches. In the nineteenth century a local solicitor, Joseph Moore, converted the land into a pleasure garden called Temple Gardens after the Greek-style temple he built overlooking the slope. A statue of Niobe – in mythology a ruler's daughter who lost her many children to vengeful deities – adorns its roof. In 1861 the month-long 'Lincoln Exhibition' here attracted 30,000 visitors. The gardens closed three years later.

There is a question mark over the Usher Gallery's future, which at the time of writing is unresolved.

Usher Gallery.

Temple in gallery grounds (1834).

45. County Offices

Between Newland and West Parade is the Lincolnshire County Council building, otherwise known as County Offices. Opened in October 1932 for 'Lindsey County Council', Henry Gamble – the retiring county architect – designed the building in the Renaissance style along simple lines and without unnecessary ornamentation. Comprising two quadrangles, the West Parade side incorporated a remnant portion of Newland House, a desirable late Georgian residence, which in the 1830s was a 'young ladies boarding school'. (Thirty years later Newland House was the property of industrialist Nathaniel Clayton, who hosted horticultural shows there.)

County Offices dates to 1932.

Lord Heneage, the council's chairman, was presented with a silver casket and key as part of the opening ceremony. One feature of the building was a new Council Chamber, for councillors to hold their committee and public meetings. Here, the acoustics were given special consideration, including placing 'eel grass' (made from seaweed) behind the panels to absorb sound vibration and prevent echoing distortion during charged debates.

In 1932, the staff's most pressing responsibility was issuing motor licences and dealing with road taxation. Today, this building is the epicentre of local government for the non-metropolitan county, its surrounding campus handling services of all types, from heritage to adult social care, childcare to traffic light regulation, pothole damage claims to school admissions and appeals. The County Council is made up of seventy councillors, representing all parts of Lincolnshire, who are elected every four years along political party allegiances. Noisy demonstrations outside County Offices – including a climate change protest in May 2019 that followed on from a national wave – are not unknown.

On the other side of Orchard Street is City Hall, seat of Lincoln City Council, which is responsible for Lincoln itself. This is a much newer building than County Offices, but has an incredible feature, in that a portion of the Roman lower town's defensive West Gate wall runs beneath it. This was built from the late second century onwards but only excavated in 1971, before City Hall was built.

This portion is much older, however, formerly being part of Newland House.

Roman wall excavated beneath City Hall.

46. RAF Skellingthorpe Bomb Store

Until comparatively recently, the land between Skellingthorpe Moor and the former Hartsholme Hall estate consisted of nothing more than open fields and parcels of woodland. Following the onset of the Second World War this expanse was developed into a sprawling Royal Air Force base, which opened in late 1941. At the time, the land fell within the parish of Skellingthorpe – hence RAF Skellingthorpe and not RAF Lincoln – with the base becoming home to the bombers and crews of 50 and 61 Squadrons.

During the war almost 2,000 men were killed flying from the airfield, including twenty-year-old Leslie Manser, Flying Officer, who sacrificed himself to save his crew during the first 'Thousand Bomber' raid of the war upon Cologne, Germany. Added to this, there were catastrophic accidents on the ground too, in 1944 and 1945, not to mention the constant threat of attack by German bombers passing overhead.

RAF Skellingthorpe closed on 31 October 1945. Plans for a Lincoln Municipal Airport were proposed in 1947 but came to nothing, and the airfield slowly reverted to agriculture. However, prefabricated Nissen huts on Skellingthorpe Road became occupied by local families, and in the early 1970s the Birchwood Housing Estate developed on the site, which by then fell within Lincoln's city boundary. Older residents still recall the airbase's empty Control Tower standing, before it made way for the Birchwood Junior School.

Virtually nothing of RAF Skellingthorpe remains. However, situated on the A46 Bypass' western side can be found portions of the base's bomb storage buildings. Today, it is difficult to appreciate that these overgrown ruins formed the western perimeter of a town-sized airbase from which – within living memory – war was organised.

Above: RAF Skellingthorpe memorial. The control tower was just over the road.

Below: Remains of RAF Skellingthorpe's component store.

47. Priory City of Lincoln Academy

This educational facility opened on Skellingthorpe Road in 1968. Originally called the City School, it replaced an older City School building situated on Monks Road, which had opened in 1886 as the School of Science & Art (and is now used by Lincoln College, called the Gibney Building).

Its pupils were boys only initially, although in 1974 it became a Comprehensive School catering for boys and girls. The school operated a traditional 'house' system, each student being allocated on their arrival to either St Hugh, Franklin, Newton or Tennyson, as an aid to team interaction. In the 1980s there was something of TV's *Grange Hill* about the place. Former pupils nowadays relate anecdotes that would be familiar to that generation the country over: of trips to Calais, children having to share the first computers, annual drama performances, cross-country runners pushing each other into Swanpool's Catchwater Drain, and of the smokers conglomerating in huge groups out of sight during break.

Many from the era may recall the Urn, a huge Grecian-style bowl stood on a solid plinth near the headmaster's office. Pupils caught fighting were often made to stand beside this ornament as a punishment, the idea being that during lessons change half the school would observe the offender stood there,

Entrance to the original City School on Monks Road.

The Urn, from Skellingthorpe Road.

who in turn would be ashamed of their behavior. This didn't necessarily have the desired effect, though, for students at the Urn often became folk heroes and momentarily 'famous'. The Urn is no longer used, and sits outside, visible from Skellingthorpe Road.

The school became an academy – the Priory City of Lincoln Academy – in 2008 and thereafter underwent an extensive redevelopment that modernised and transformed the look of the old 1968 'City School' entirely.

48. Lincoln Drill Hall

There is a dramatic contrast between the two entrances to the Drill Hall.

The Broadgate side clearly reflects its origins. Presented to the city by Joseph Ruston, it was built with a military aspect, including embattlements and watch turret, for the 1st Lincolnshire Volunteer Battalion. It also had a 62-foot by 15-foot armoury and adjoining ammunition store. Opened on 24 May 1890 by

Above left: Drill Hall, from Broadgate.

Above right: Drill Hall, from Free School Lane.

the Secretary of State for War, its original function was as a base for military training and exercise; however, a fully fitted soup kitchen was also incorporated, in case poverty or famine struck Lincolnshire. The building's architect was Major F. H. Goddard, of Lincoln.

During Lincoln's typhoid epidemic of 1904/05 the Drill Hall was used as a hospital for those affected, with horse-drawn ambulances a common sight outside. By this time it was being used for flower shows, and over time moved into public use as a venue. There were jazz concerts in the 1940s, and the Rolling Stones even performed there on New Year's Eve 1963. Today, it is home to the annual Lincoln Beer Festival.

When it reopened on 20 March 2004 following a £3 million refurbishment, it was also as a modern performing arts venue. A new entrance from Free School Lane now boasts a 15-foot metal sculpture shaped like a human face, designed by Hertfordshire artist Rick Kirby – effectively advertising the hall's contemporary purpose. In 2015, commemorative stones were unveiled beneath this artwork in memory of two Lincoln men who received the Victoria Cross for valour during the First World War.

49. The Engine Shed

Between the Rope Walk and the Brayford Pool is the University of Lincoln. This was officially opened in 1996 by Queen Elizabeth II, becoming Lincoln's newest public university (after Bishop Grosseteste University, which had been established in the 1860s as a teacher training college). Since its inception, Lincoln University has only flourished in scope and reputation.

On the campus, the Engine Shed – Lincoln's biggest live music and entertainment venue – was born in 2006, following the £6 million renovation of a disused,

Above: Engine Shed.

Below: The defunct East Holmes signal box next to the Students' Union Tower Bar.

multi-track railway storage facility dating to 1875 connected with the old Holmes Yard. Sitting adjacent on the campus is the University Library – another former railway building, the 1907 Great Central Warehouse.

As of 2014, the University of Lincoln Students' Union has operated the Engine Shed, which is sandwiched between the Lincoln Performing Arts Centre and the Students' Union Tower Bar. The Engine Shed can pack in over 1,500 people, and although it hosts various events, it is most famous for its live music: The Human League, The Stranglers, Manic Street Preachers, Stereophonics, Ellie Goulding, Kings of Leon, Pixie Lott, Dizzee Rascal, Florence and the Machine, Kaiser Chiefs and Kasabian are just some of the big-name acts to have performed there.

5c. Waterside Shopping Centre

Musically, the Engine Shed's success recalls the 1960s, when Lincoln hosted equally big names: Cilla Black; the Kinks; the Who; the Moody Blues; and of course, the Beatles in November 1963, who legendarily performed at the Savoy Theatre, or ABC. Someone who was there, then aged thirteen, tells me, 'There was

Waterside Shopping Centre; the white building is the former Saracen's Head.

Millennium sculpture on the shopping centre's south side.

so much screaming that you couldn't actually hear them play anything. Girls in the crowd were fainting, and some had to be carried out.' Lincoln, it seems, was no different to anywhere else in becoming gripped by 'Beatlemania'.

From 1936 long queues for the Savoy regularly formed along Saltergate; but the venue no longer exists, for it was demolished in April 1990 (along with a large Woolworths store, which had opened in 1924) for the Waterside Shopping Centre. Many will remember crowds thronging High Street to see Prince Charles and Princess Diana open the replacement shopping complex in 1992. Today this new landmark is complemented by a 2002 artwork on its southern side, arcing over the Witham: the Millennium *Empowerment* sculpture by Stephen Broadbent.

Neighbouring the Waterside Shopping Centre on the High Street, a first-floor iron balcony above Waterstones and H. Samuel evidences this was until 1959 The Saracen's Head Hotel. This had existed in some form for centuries. It was here in 1865 that prolonged election rioting started, pitting mobs against police and soldiers, and seeing Tentercroft Street barricaded. As this illustrates, history hides *everywhere* in Lincoln. A hundred other buildings – some now long gone, some hiding in plain sight, some very familiar and picturesque, and some newly erected – would have made worthy, interesting additions to this work in their own right. This author was once told that, to understand Lincoln's history, one had to continually *look one storey up* as they explored. It is a truism. Any visitor to Lincoln can be assured that the more they look, the more they'll see.

Picturesque Lincoln – Michaelgate's Crooked House.

Acknowledgements

Rich Storey, Mayor's Officer, City of Lincoln Council, for his help in researching the Guildhall's medieval gaol and Lincoln's first bank; Zena Herring and Owen Teather, for use of early twentieth-century photographs and pictures, personally taken and collected in the private family album of William Barnes (William, an early amateur photographer, retired in 1945 after fifty-one years as an engineer, designer and international sales rep for Rustons); Kate Fenn, Civic & International Partnerships Manager, City of Lincoln Council; Brian Taylor, Lincoln Guildhall Tour Guide, for his experience and knowledge; The Collection (Art and Archaeology in Lincolnshire) for permission to use photos of exhibits; Lincoln Cathedral Communications and Marketing. All photos relating to Lincoln Castle's interior and antiquities are used courtesy of Lincolnshire County Council. All information herein has been sourced from an amalgamation of antiquarian studies, city histories, museum exhibits, tourism information, maps of various eras, local galleries, personal knowledge and local first-hand accounts, and cross-referenced as thoroughly as possible.